KU-130-666

BETWEEN
THE
SEAS

Christopher Thorne died soon after completing *Between the Seas*. He was known as a distinguished academic, historian and expert on international relations, but I think that he put as much passion into this book on Crete as into any of his works of history. It is a very personal book, and exudes energy, love of physical action, and sense of place in every sentence. Above all, it embodies Christopher's gregariousness, his enthusiasm for people. It is not an important book, but it was intensely important to him. It is sad that he did not live to see it published.

Christopher Sinclair-Stevenson

BETWEEN THE SEAS

A Quiet Walk Through Crete

CHRISTOPHER
THORNE

SINCLAIR-STEVENSON

First published in Great Britain by
Sinclair-Stevenson
7/8 Kendrick Mews
London sw7 3hg, England

Copyright © 1992 by Christopher Thorne

All rights reserved. Without limiting the rights under
copyright reserved, no part of this publication may be
reproduced, stored in or introduced into a retrieval system
or transmitted, in any form or by any means (electronic,
mechanical, photocopying, recording or otherwise), without
the prior written permission of both the copyright owner
and the above publisher of this book.

The right of Christopher Thorne to be identified as author of
this work has been asserted by him in accordance with the
Copyright, Designs and Patents Act 1988.

British Library Cataloguing in Publication Data
A CIP catalogue record for this book is available from the
British Library.

isbn: 1 85619 188 5

Design & Map by Lesley Robinson

Typeset by Rowland Phototypesetting Limited
Bury St Edmunds, Suffolk

Printed and bound in Great Britain by
Clays Limited, St Ives plc

For the families Adamakis and Parasiris,
who have done so much to foster my love of Crete
and who provided encouragement and assistance for the walk itself;
and for my granddaughter, Naomi, who, then nearly new,
accompanied me on that walk in photographic form.

VANGELIS ADAMAKIS

ELOUNDA

P.O. BOX. 6

CRETE - GREECE

'The proud, wild, and lordly island.'

Nikos Kazantzakis,
Zorba The Greek

Για τούτο οπού 'ναι φρόνιμος, μηδέ χαθή στα πάθη·
το ρόδο κι όμορφος αθός γεννάται μες στ' αγκάθι . . .
Και κάθα είς που εδιάβασεν εδά κι ας το κατέχη:
μη χάνεται στα κίντυνα, μα πάντα ολπίδα ας έχη.

From the *Erotokritos*,
by the Cretan poet Vitsentzos Kornaros*

*Therefore, whosoever is wise, let him not waste away in sufferings;
the rose, lovely flower, is born among thorns . . .
So let everyone who has read this now understand:
let him not waste away in adversity but always have hope.

Quoted and translated by David Holton in his (edited)
Literature and Society in Renaissance Crete (Cambridge, 1991)

Contents

Preface

What follows is an account of a single walk through Crete, which lasted for a mere two weeks. It also contains reflections on aspects of the island's life and history, as they arise along the line of the walk itself. In other words, this short book is in no way intended as a survey of Crete as a whole, for many parts of the island, together with many facets of its rich past, are left aside. Nor is the book to be seen as a detailed guide for those visitors to Crete who possess the inclination and the capacity to take to its mountains on foot. For me, walking is a very personal matter – not only where I go, but also how I go there – and I imagine it is the same for many others. If there are practical lessons to be found in these pages – including, of course, lessons to be drawn from mistakes on my part – and if others find them useful in the future, I shall be glad. But my intention has lain elsewhere: simply, by relating this single journey, to attempt to convey something of my own long-standing love of the island, its mountains, and its people, together with the exhilaration which they have fostered in me over the years.

Perhaps I should add a brief explanation of the book's subtitle, since a journey that involved walking and climbing an average of about 30 miles a day for a fortnight, crossing mountains in temperatures of around 90 to 100 degrees and with over 30 lbs on one's back, may not at first sight seem an obvious way of achieving quietude. But the entire experience did bring quietness with it, in two respects. First, I was for the most part entirely alone with the wind and the olive groves and the mountains. And second, physical endeavours notwithstanding, I felt extremely tranquil throughout. In this connection, too, I would echo Jonathan Raban's observation, made in the context of his splendid account of his journey down the Mississippi, *Old Glory*, that 'There always comes a point in travelling when motion itself has become so habitual that it breeds its own deep stillness.'

I must express my warm thanks to a number of friends who in a variety of ways have helped to make this book possible. The enormous debt that I owe to the Adamakis and Parasiris families in Crete itself is reflected in the dedication and will also become apparent in the account that follows. I must make special mention of Vangelis Adamakis' readiness to answer a stream of questions from me over the years, not least when I began drafting this book.

The hospitality and encouragement of many other Cretans have been central to my experience of the island, and again several of those involved will make their appearance in the ensuing pages. I should like to make particular mention, though, of Nikos Paterakis, retired sea-captain and *bon viveur*, who has joined Vangelis Adamakis in patiently developing my ability to get by in Greek. Two of my Greek students at the University of Sussex, Lefki Dimoulas and Pandelis Sklias, have both helped me to increase my understanding of their country as a whole and its society, the latter readily undertaking the additional task of assisting me to derive full benefit from the second, untranslated volume of S. G. Spanakis' work, *Η ΚΡΗΤΗ: ΤΟΥΡΙΣΤΙΚΟΣ ΙΣΤΟΡΙΚΟΣ ΑΡΧΑΙΟΛΟΓΙΚΟΣ: ΟΔΗΓΟΣ.*

My colleagues in the Library of the University of Sussex have been as unfailingly helpful as ever, and I should particularly like to thank David Kennelly and Joan Benning in this connection. Sue Murray-Smith, my secretary, has furnished assistance far beyond the typing of the manuscript, while my publisher and friend of over twenty years, Christopher Sinclair-Stevenson, has once again been the ideal promoter and facilitator of the enterprise.

I am most grateful to a number of other friends who have found the time to read the book in draft form and to offer helpful comments: Gabriel Josipovici, Nigel Llewellyn, Mark Mazower, Gotthold Müller, René Weis and Ian Young. I leave until last my beloved partner, Iz, who, quite apart from climbing with me in Crete and commenting on the typescript, has provided support that is not to be defined in mere words.

CHRISTOPHER THORNE
Elounda and Brighton, 1991

Note on transliteration

I am comforted to know that those far more expert than I find this a problem when rendering Greek into English. I have no doubt that there exist excellent schemes that could be followed in this regard, but here I have simply tried in my own fashion to get somewhere near the sounds in question. There are good arguments both for and against including accents; I have left them out.

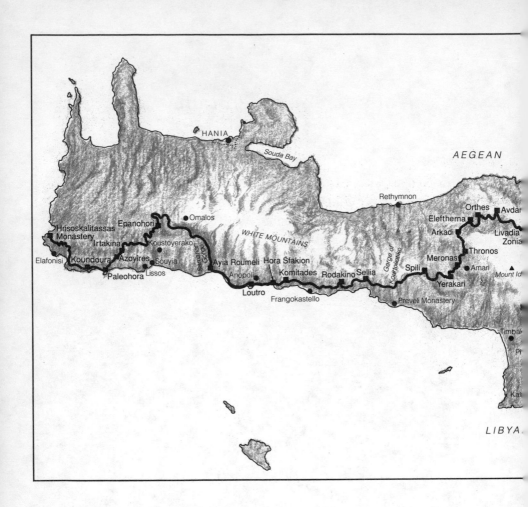

AEGEAN

LIBYA

HANIA

Souda Bay

Rethymnon

Orthes
Avdar
Eleftherna
Livadia
Arkadi
Zonia
Thronos
Meronas
Spili
Amari
Yerakari
Mount Id

WHITE MOUNTAINS

Omalos

Epanohori
Hrisoskalitassas
Monastery
Irtakina
Koustoyerako
Elafonisi
Azoyires
Koundoura
Souyia
Ayia Roumeli
Hora Sfakion
Paleohora
Lissos
Anopoli
Komitades
Rodakino
Sellia
Loutro
Frangokastello
Preveli Monastery

Gorge of Kourtoliako

Timbai
Pr
Kal

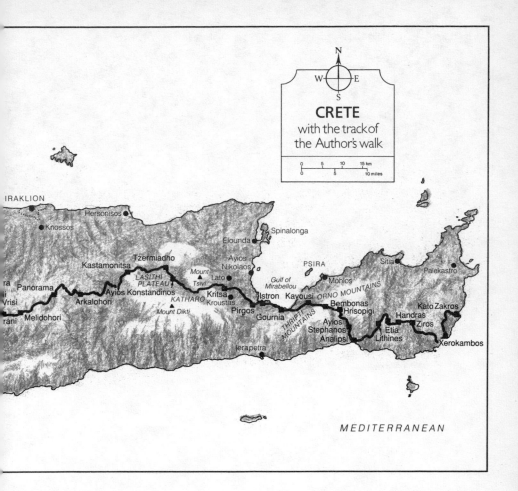

CRETE
with the track of
the Author's walk

N
W · E
S

| 0 | 5 | 10 | 15 km |
| 0 | | 5 | 10 miles |

IRAKLION

Hersonisos

Knossos

Spinalonga

Elounda

Ayios
Nikolaos

PSIRA

Sitia

Tzermiadho

Kastamonitsa

*LASITHI
PLATEAU*

Mount
Tsivi

Lato

*Gulf of
Mirabellou*

Mohlos

ORNO MOUNTAINS

Palekastro

Panorama

Ayios Konstandinos

Kritsa

Ilstron

Kavousi

Bembonas

Kato Zakros

ra
i
Vrisi

Arkalohori

KATHARO

Kroustas

Hrisopigi

Handras

Melidohori

ráni

Mount Dikti

Pirgos

Gournia

*THRIPTI
MOUNTAINS*

Ayios
Stephanos

Analipsi

Etia

Lithines

Ziros

Xerokambos

Ierapetra

MEDITERRANEAN

CHAPTER ONE

The island and the idea

One hot afternoon in the summer of 1989, I lay on a beach near the small village of Lenika, in north-eastern Crete, and formulated a question that was to buzz around in my head for the next year or so. Would it be possible, I wondered, for me to walk, on my own, from one end of the island to the other, keeping away from metalled roads for the most part, while zigzagging in order to traverse all of the main mountain ranges along the way?

A number of Cretan friends had done much to bring me to the point where I could dare to contemplate such a venture, as I shall recall in a moment. But it was a friend from England, Peter Sissons, who unwittingly brought the idea to the fore amid the lazy setting of the beach that day, when he happened to remark that his brother John had once purchased a donkey in Sitia, towards the north-east corner of the island, and with this beast as his porter had journeyed on foot as far as Rethymnon, to the west of centre along the island's northern shore. I myself had become accustomed to walking considerable distances in the Cretan sun in that part of the country where I was then staying. I had climbed, too, the summit of the island's highest peak, Mount Ida (to the natives, 'Psiloritis'), by way of the towering waves of often-loose rock that constitute its northern face. Whether I could sustain such journeyings day after day, however, and over hundreds of miles, was another matter altogether. But once the project was lodged in my mind, it had to be attempted.

Thirteen months later, after travelling for two weeks across the island and its mountains, I arrived at a remote monastery on the western shore. My walking-boots, together with the feet inside them, were somewhat battered, but I had undergone a unique and thrilling experience: one that I was sure would remain vivid and significant throughout the remainder of my life. I had

1

learnt some things about myself, perhaps; certainly I had learnt more about the 'proud, wild, and lordly island' that is Crete. And because that island (and not, say, Tuscany, or the Pyrenees, as it might have been) had provided the inspiration and the challenge for the walk, I should begin, before narrating the journey itself, by trying to explain briefly why that was so: why not only the topography but also the equally remarkable history and society of Crete bore the chief responsibility for goading me towards the achievement of a fine set of blisters and a great exhilaration.

Crete has long been a cradle of freedom. A land that can enslave by its own beauty, the 'Great Island' has nurtured a people who remain characterised, in Dilys Powell's words, by 'an air of inherent independence'. 'No people has ever been more individualistic', reflected A. M. (Sandy) Rendel, diplomatic correspondent of *The Times*, after his service alongside local partisans during the brutal German occupation of 1941–45. 'No people has ever been more litigious, more lively, or above all more devoted to pulling its own leg.' These qualities, as he saw it, all 'dated from ancient days', and they made resistance to the latest in a long line of oppressors 'a personal and passionate emotion'.

These are generalisations, of course, of a kind that we all resort to when seeking to convey the essence or the feel of a society. They were put forward by observers who knew very well that there had been a number of Cretans ready to betray their fellow countrymen to the Germans during the Second World War, just as there had been during the preceding centuries a good many who found it convenient to convert to the Islamic faith when the island lay under Turkish occupation, some of them obediently taking up arms in the Turkish cause against the uprisings of their fellow Greeks. As for the glories of Minoan Crete, they sprang, after all, from a society in which both slavery and serfdom had their place.

Even so, the generalisations may stand, and it is no chance matter that the very word for freedom, 'eleftheria', has been widely employed in Crete as a Christian name – as in the case, for example, of that great twentieth-century Greek statesman, Venizelos. The summary of the Cretan character recently drawn up by Antony Beevor in his history of the island's battles during the Second World War[1] may not fit all those natives who now seek to make a living from the annual tourist invasion of the northern shore (indeed, cynicism and exploitation are not unknown in those surroundings); but up in the mountain regions, especially, 'warlike, proud, compulsively generous to a friend or stranger in need, ferociously unforgiving to an enemy or traitor, frugal day by day but prodigal in celebration' – such terms retain their validity. The spirit that was manifested at the Arkadi Monastery in 1866, where, as I shall go on to relate in more detail, over 800 men, women and children died rather than surrender to the besieging Turks, has not yet succumbed to the islanders' changing life styles. And for those wanting more recent examples of such defiance in the cause of freedom, Beevor's own book gives an account of that remarkable episode at Galatas on 22 May 1941, when a motley collection of primitively armed old men, women and children charged, shouting, over open ground and into the sights of soon-faltering German airborne units who had come to seize the island for the Third Reich.[2]

The generalisations about the Cretan's individualism and love of freedom can be sustained, then. So, too, can those broad assertions that stress the significance of the island in the development of European civilisation. In effect, writes Paul Faure in his detailed account of life in Minoan times, 'Europe begins here', and in search of a greater understanding of why that is so I long

[1] See the bibliographical note for details of this and other books cited in the text.

[2] Lawrence Durrell, in his book *The Greek Islands*, illustrates the extremities to which pride in one's courage can be taken. 'During a [World War Two] parachute course in the Middle East the instructor, jump-training a group of commandos from various islands, saw one of them fumble with his harness and hesitate to advance into the bay for the jump. Incautiously, he made a pleasantry – asking if the novice was scared. The response was unexpected. "Scared?" cried the young man, "You dare to tell a Cretan that he is scared? I'll show you who is scared." He unhooked his safety harness altogether and jumped to his certain death.'

ago dutifully joined the throng of visitors to Knossos and (less crowded and more beautifully set on its hillside) Phaestos. It is exciting, of course, to stand upon such sites, as it is to recall Homer's famous lines in *The Odyssey* about the island's 'ninety cities'. (Faure lists ninety-three that have pre-Hellenic names.) For me, though, the immense richness of Cretan history – the post-Minoan mark left by the Dorians in cities like Lato, for example, or the later significance of the island within Byzantium, above all as the 'citadel of Hellenism' after the fall of Constantinople in 1453 – has been brought home only through a close acquaintance with the land itself.

The land and the sea together, that is, for the two are both historically and topographically inseparable. Crete's 'rich and lovely terrain', wrote Homer, is 'washed by the waves on every side.' The Poseidon myth; the sailor-as-peasant; the sea as a bridge to be crossed for the enlargement of Minoan wealth: these and other aspects of the symbiosis have been explored by Faure and others. And for a time, at least, the surrounding seas did serve both to protect the island and to enhance its fortunes. Crete, observed Aristotle in his *Politics*, 'seems to be intended by nature for dominion in Hellas, and to be well situated; it extends right across the sea round which nearly all the Hellenes are settled; and while one end is not far from the Peloponnese, the other almost reaches to regions of Asia . . . Hence Minos acquired the empire of the sea. . . .' Nearly two millennia later, in 1589, a Venetian nobleman was moved to a more lyrical description still, concerning an island that was 'one of the most famous in the world, . . . ly[ing] in the centre of the Mediterranean, or rather in the middle of the world, since it is equidistant from Asia, Africa, and Europe. . . . It deserves,' he concluded, 'to become the capital of the world.'

By then, of course, the sea had become less of a moat than a highway for invaders – not least for the Venetians themselves, who emblazoned the lion of Saint Mark upon Crete's few fortresses, and who sought to suppress the rebellious natives, fellow Christians or no, with a ferocity that at times outdid the harshness of the Mohammedan Turk who followed. Even so, the contributions that the island had already made to the political and cultural development of Europe were indelible – and indeed, in the eyes of the US Consul there in the 1860s, Crete's subsequent removal from the centre to the periphery of affairs was itself to be seen as a blessing. (The island possessed, he argued, 'one of those paradisical isolations which facilitate civilization in its early stages and preserve it from the encroachments of progress in the later.') Certainly, whether under the dominion of Frank[1] or pasha, the people of Crete themselves did not lose their strong love of their motherland (the female identification was marked), a feature of the society that impressed itself upon visitors like Edward Lear, for example, who arrived in 1864 to potter resolutely around the island's western and central areas, sketching as he went.

Lear was inclined to grumble at first: Crete, he decided, possessed only limited attractions, and although it was spring the sun only occasionally showed itself, with clouds sitting heavily upon Mount Ida. '*All* Crete is mountain,' observed the fussily tenacious bachelor. (He was fifty-two at the time.) But by the end of his visit, for all the grey skies and the vermin and the waywardness of his hired muleteer, he was in better spirits – not simply as a consequence of the copious use of flea-powder, but because the island's beauty had at last claimed him as an admirer. As for the natives' own keen awareness of that beauty, their celebrated novelist Nikos Kazantzakis spoke for many, down to the present day, through the mouth of his hero Captain Michalis:[2]

> 'How beautiful Crete,' he murmured, 'how beautiful! Ah! If only I were an eagle, to admire the whole of Crete from an airy height!' And truly an

[1] That is, more northern and western Europeans of a non-Orthodox religious persuasion.

[2] This particular novel of Kazantzakis, as translated into English by Jonathan Griffin, is entitled (not without poetic justification) *Freedom and Death*. The original, however, takes as its title the long-standing Cretan slogan, 'freedom *or* death': *Ελευθερια η θανατος*.

eagle would see beauties to admire in Crete. The way its close-knit body rose and poised, sun-browned, the way its coasts gleamed, now with white sand, now with blood-red, sheer promontories. He must needs rejoice over the villages, the big farms, and the little churches glittering against the iron-dark rock or planted deep in the soil. . . .'

For those not blessed with the eagle's vantage-point, Crete, for all the forbidding nature of its terrain, has since Minoan times offered the traveller a network of tracks and dirt-roads that link the island from end to end. And in modern – though pre-tourist – times, no one did more to explore and make use of such by-ways than the British archaeologist, John Pendlebury: not simply a Cretophile, but in effect 'Kritikos', a Cretan man; scholarly guide to the island's archaeological riches; athlete (he had been a Cambridge high jumper) who raced across its mountains and through its ravines; lover of freedom who died – murdered in cold blood by the Germans – after being wounded in the fight for the island in 1941.

Pendlebury concluded the Introduction to his book, *The Archaeology of Crete*, by celebrating, in terms that I can do no more than echo, the joys of walking and climbing around the island amid the company of its shepherds and villagers:

'To have stood on Ida, on Dikte and on Aphendes-Kavousi in the clear shrill wind and to have toiled through the hot little valleys with that unforgettable smell of herbs is an experience the memory of which nothing can take away from you.'

In wider terms, his suggestion to those who wished to get to know Greece in general was simple and (as Dilys Powell has emphasised) of lasting value:

'Our last advice is, learn a word or two of modern Greek, think of a nice-sounding name, look it up on the map and go there. Take to the hills and

thank heaven for the fine tall gentlemen you meet.
Eat and drink with them; ask what they think of
the ruins and their history; and in a week you will
learn more about Greece than twenty people who
have motored everywhere for a month.'

Another of the great British lovers and knowers of Crete, Patrick
Leigh Fermor – his name still conjured with around a shepherd's
fire on the mountain plain of Katharo or in the cool of a cheese-
making hut above Kastamonitsa – has also succeeded in capturing
in words something of the sensations to be gained from such
journeying on foot, especially if undertaken alone. Thus, of his
passage through the Carpathian uplands, during his 1930s walk
from the Hook of Holland to Constantinople, he writes in
Between the Woods and the Water:

'Starting at dawn, ending at dark, and only separ-
ated by light sleep, each day in the mountains
seemed to contain a longer sequence of phases than
a week at ground level. Twenty-four hours would
spin themselves into a lifetime, and thin mountain
air, sharpened faculties, the piling-up of detail and
a kaleidoscope of scene-changes seemed to turn the
concatenation into a kind of eternity. I felt deeply
involved in these dizzying solitudes, more reluctant each minute to come down again and ready to
go on forever.'

I suppose that to think and feel in such terms is to join the late
Bruce Chatwin in believing that 'walking is not simply thera-
peutic for oneself but is a poetic activity' – though I hesitate over
his accompanying assertion that such activity 'can cure the world
of its ills'. 'Walking is virtue, tourism deadly sin.' The aphorism
produced by Chatwin's friend Werner Herzog also seems to me
somewhat ponderous and overstated, but again the underlying
notion to my mind has some validity.

I arrived in Crete for the first time in the early 1980s on a package-holiday, but quickly took off independently in order to explore the island's roads (both metalled and dirt) by car. I found myself captivated by the land and its people. Over the years my work as an international historian, as well as travel embarked upon purely for pleasure, had taken me to many parts of the world – within India and Japan, for example – that were not only beautiful but also fascinating for historical or sociological reasons. And there were other far-away regions, such as the south island of New Zealand, which I particularly wanted to explore further on foot. But the topography, history, and people of Crete attracted me to a degree that was new in my experience.

And so I returned in the following years to spend as much of each summer there as possible, taking with me the writing tasks that could now be pursued only during the long vacation of my university, following the degradations of the Thatcher years. A circle of Cretan friends and acquaintances widened *pari passu* with the radius of my walks – walks that were initially undertaken with a degree of unpreparedness that I look back upon as utter foolishness. For example, I wound my way from Kritsa, through the pleasant villages of Kroustas and Prina, then down to the southern coast across the less-than-lovely plain around Ierapetra, wearing on my feet only a pair of sandals, and with pads of steadily hardening cotton-wool – not the soft lambswool that I now carry with me – held on by cellotape over the inevitably ensuing blisters. The faces of some of the village men as I passed by were, I remember, mutely eloquent on the subject of eccentric urban amateurs.

The dawn ascent of Oxa, the peak that hangs above the village of Elounda in the north-east of the island, became a frequent delight, providing a fine vantage-point from which to watch the sun come flooding across the Gulf of Mirabellou. On the opposite side of that bay, the peak of Papoura, reached by a long, steady climb through the coniferous woods below the decaying village of Thripti, gave me an even more spectacular view – back across the water towards Ayios Nikolaos and the village of Lenika where I was living. With much improved footwear and, I think, a growing feel for the countryside, I began what became the fairly frequent exercise of climbing up from Kritsa, above Ayios Nikolaos, to the Lasithi Plateau: by the easy way along the dirt-road that winds up to the tranquil plain of Katharo, then over the rim of Lasithi's own (lower) bowl and down into Ayios Konstandinos; or by a more gruelling route, along the dried river-bed from Kritsa to Tapes, then up a steep ravine above that latter village, across the shoulder of Mount Tsivi, and gently down to join the road from Neapolis as it drops into the Lasithi plain.

But these were all local walks, and expeditions and bases further afield were needed if I was to get to grips with more of the island than the nomos, or province, of Lasithi itself. Walks down the famous gorge of Samaria in the south-west, organised independently of tour-groups, helped to whet my appetite, even though the increasing number of tourists making the descent – bunched together in the early stages and with a good many choosing to chatter their way down – took the edge off that particular pleasure as the years passed. More challenging by far, in any case, were the exercises that resulted from my making new shepherd friends – above all the extensive Parasiris family – in the mountain village of Zoniana. For these new expeditions included the ascent of the neighbouring Mount Ida, or Psiloritis, the highest mountain in the island, and this in the company of shepherds almost half my age who strolled these precipitous slopes on legs like steel springs while going about their daily work.

Other new friends, meanwhile, were playing their part in sharpening my imagination and appetite. Yannis Dafermos, for example, coffee-house owner, barber and lira-player in the historically important village of Axos, close to Zoniana, who would close his kafeneion in order to play and sing undisturbed, and whose long, printed poem on the destruction of nearby Anoyia by the Germans in 1944 served as a sharp reminder that, however much my ability to converse in Greek was improving, my knowledge of the language was still primitive. George Psychoundakis was another, though I met him only once: famed for his wartime exploits with the partisans and for his moving account of them in *The Cretan Runner*, translated into English by his friend Leigh

Fermor; warm in his greeting of a complete stranger, and helpful in directing me to the spot where another wartime hero, the New Zealander Dudley Perkins (of whom more follows) had been ambushed and killed.

And so I was brought to the state that enabled an ambition to traverse the island on foot to emerge in the front of my mind that afternoon in 1989 on the beach near Lenika. There would be an obvious starting point for such a journey at its eastern end in the shape of Kato Zakros, the site of a not-long-discovered Minoan palace by the water's edge. The final destination also required little thought: the monastery of the Golden Stairway, Hrisoskalitissas, perched on its rock above the sea at the westernmost tip of the island. I had visited this remote establishment by car several years earlier with one of my daughters, there to meet the unforgettable Sister Theodoti Kolokotronis, who remained the solitary nun living in the building, her vital personality belying her eighty or so years and defying a crippling of the knee-joints that made it so difficult for her to negotiate the stone stairways of the monastery she cherished.

There it was, then. Could I, in a single journey, walk across the mountains of Crete, between the seas, to pay another visit to Theodoti Kolokotronis? At this early stage of the project, a year in advance, I confided only in my Cretan mentor, Vangelis Adamakis. He was prepared, after some reflection, to deliver himself of the opinion that he thought me both strong enough and mad enough at least to have a shot at the task – even if I persisted, against his advice, in my plan to make the attempt during the heat of summer. (By the time I had completed my training and acclimatisation in Crete itself, the latter part of August and early September would be the only period available to me.)

I also undertook there and then, in the late summer of 1989, a few further exploratory journeys with the larger project in mind: for example, climbing over the easternmost mountain barrier behind Kato Zakros (a tougher one than it seemed at first glance) to the small town of Ziros beyond. This particular day's exercise was complicated by buses that ran late; by an acute thirst brought on less by temperatures in the nineties (to which I'd long become accustomed) than by the decision to take kaolin-and-morphine tablets in order to calm an upset stomach – another lesson learned; and by the hospitality of villagers beyond Ziros, who insisted that I consume on the spot handfuls of the grapes that they were harvesting – thereby threatening to undermine the more beneficent effects of the aforesaid kaolin and morphine and obliging me to jog the final three miles or so in order to reach the hamlet of Papagiannades in time to catch the infrequent bus that would take me to Ierapetra, and there to a connection back across to the north coast and home. This particular expedition also led to the decision that I would begin the longer journey the following year, not by assaulting the eastern mountains by the narrow track I had sought to follow that day (it had become so overgrown that I had lost it, and been left to make my way over the thorn-clad mountain-side), but by following the dirt-road that ran further south before crossing the barrier by a series of goose-neck twists that would better suit the load I would then be carrying.

During the ensuing winter and spring, the projected walk amid the heat and rocks of Crete provided a new, long-term purpose for my usual exercising among the soft green folds of the South Downs. Indeed, the thought of what lay ahead prompted me to undertake repeated ascents and descents of the steeper scarps of those great whalebacks, as Kipling called them, and to complete the seventy-four miles between Eastbourne and Petersfield over a brisk couple of days.

But Crete itself, I knew, was where I must ensure that my preparations were adequate for the task I'd set myself. Each day during July and early August 1990, therefore, before settling down to academic work in my rented apartment in Elounda, I engaged in some mild climbing at dawn, together with a kind of loping run – the best that could be managed over the rocky tracks or hillsides – on the nearby large island of Spinalonga (not to be confused with its small neighbour of that name, famous for its remains of both a Venetian fortress and a leper colony). There is far more countryside – and there are far more toiling hills –

contained within Spinalonga than many realise who sail by it on their way to its picturesque satellite; far more ruined dwellings, too, hidden away among its folds. Indeed, the invaluable record made by Robert Pashley, Fellow of Trinity College, Cambridge, after his 1834 visit to Crete tells us that in that year there were no less than eighty-one families living on Spinalonga, all of them Muslim, incidentally.[1]

As the date for beginning the walk drew closer – I'd settled on Sunday 19th August, after working backwards from the time when I would have to leave the island to return to Britain – I decided to give my stamina and climbing-muscles a final checkout on the nearby and familiar peak of Oxa (known in the 1860s, according to that cheerful traveller, Captain. T. A. B. Spratt, RN, CB, FRS, as 'Oxah or Axos' and featuring along its narrow crowning ridge a row of water cisterns the remains of which are still visible today[2]). In order to ensure that the test would involve lifting a greater load than I would have to shoulder on the walk itself, I settled on the maximum airline-baggage weight of 20 kgs or 44 lbs. A few large rocks placed inside a plastic bucket served the purpose, the bucket in turn fitting into my rucksack. The straps creaked, as did my thigh-muscles to begin with, and as I climbed up towards the peak for the first time via the track that runs steeply up behind Elounda, I wondered if I'd taken on too much. But I soon became accustomed to the load, even though it forced my legs from under me a couple of times during descents among the loose rocks that adorn the Lenika face of the mountain. Seven very hot hours later, with more lessons learned, four ascents and four descents behind me, and a few large thorn spikes

[1] This does not necessarily mean that they were Turkish. They may well have been among those Greeks who, as mentioned earlier, found it expedient to convert to Islam during the Turkish occupation. Many villages in Crete at the time had a clear leaning one way or the other. Thus, Kritsa, not far from Spinalonga, had 180 Christian and only 2 Muslim families in 1834. Others, however, were able to exist on a more ambivalent basis, with Ziros having 30 families of each of the two religious persuasions and a smaller hamlet like Thronos, 9 Christian and 6 Muslim.

[2] Legend has it that one cistern was, and remains, filled with gold. A number of my local friends have already claimed their share of the proceeds in return for having given me this priceless information and in the confident expectation that I shall one day come across the treasure during my frequent prowlings around the peak.

embedded in my wrists, I was back in the bath, with several pints of shandy to hand and feeling fairly confident that, mechanically at least, I was ready for the coming challenge.

Less histrionic preparations included detailed work with the best map of the island that I had been able to find – though as we shall see even this version left walkers very much to their own devices once away from the metalled roads. Nothing comparable to the British Ordnance Survey series was available, and the leading map-shops in London reported severe limitations in this regard upon what the Greek authorities would make available. (This could be due to a continuing, atavistic readiness for renewed combat with the Turk, or just as easily to sheer incompetence. One wonders if high-class, detailed maps of an area like Crete actually exist anywhere in the bureaucratic catacombs of Athens.) Having already been caught once on the summit of Ida/Psiloritis in dense cloud – even my local shepherd friends had argued fiercely between themselves (Cretans seldom argue in any other fashion, of course) over which direction to take – I made seaman-like notes of the compass-bearings I would need to follow if clouds came down again as I climbed over from Kamares to Zoniana.

Such abrupt changes of direction as the one involved in crossing over Psiloritis, together with visits such as the one I intended to make to the Arkadi monastery and the endless zigzagging of dirt-roads and mountain-tracks alike, were obviously going to add considerably to the 156 or so miles that a crow would have to cover when travelling the length of the island. My rough estimate was that the journey would be one of around 250 to 280 miles. That in turn enabled me to entertain the comfortable notion that I would need to average only about twenty a day in order to complete the walk in the fortnight that I had allowed for it, leaving a few days over at the end of my stay before returning to Britain.

This seemed a perfectly manageable task. For although I found that the weight of my pack – when fully loaded with water, basic food-supplies like cheese, glucose and nuts, with notebooks and camera, spare clothes, running shoes to wear in the evenings, toilet-gear and so on – came to around 33 lbs, this was considerably less than I had managed during my Oxa test. Moreover, I had become accustomed to exceeding by far twenty miles in a day, both in Britain and in Crete – and that without being troubled by blisters, since I had taken care to harden my feet by the regular application of surgical spirit. Even so, I would clearly need to maintain a certain momentum if I was to reach the western end of the island in a fortnight. I therefore adopted in advance the rule that while I would stop along the way to enjoy the company of Cretans, I would not do so in order to explore archaeological sites or similar points of interest – many of which were in any case already known to me, while the others could be revisited in more leisurely fashion over the years to come.

I made preparations, too, for keeping a journal, simply in order to help preserve the details and sensations of the walk. (The decision to write a book about the experience was to come later, after it was over.) I also worked harder at my Greek in the evenings. And even during the mornings I noticed that my attention was tending to slip away from the subject of the academic book I was drafting, in order to dwell on those pocket-sized and numbered sections of the map of the island that I had prepared: in particular, on those parts of my intended route that were unfamiliar to me, and the points where it would be important to find a new track or turning.

I still lacked one major item of equipment, however: a strong staff, which would be essential if I were to minimise the danger of a headlong descent while negotiating the loose rock-falls that are common on the mountain faces. Such a staff, in addition to my shepherd's knife, would also provide insurance if I happened to chance upon a wild dog or two of aggressive disposition, as I had done once in the past. But wherever I looked, the staves that were for sale failed to reach the height that my own size, together with the weight of my pack, seemed to require. It was a problem that I mentioned in all innocence when visiting the Parasiris family in Zoniana, partly in order to alert them to the fact that I hoped to be returning on foot, over the mountain, a few weeks thereafter, at what would be roughly the half-way point of the projected journey. At once Kostas, the head of the family, went to the wall and took down a magnificent shepherd's crook, or bastouni, that was hanging there. Made of wild oak from the slopes of Ida itself, it stood four feet from the ground. 'You should have this,' he said simply. And thus I came into one of my most treasured possessions.

I came, too, into what was to prove (and has continued to prove on subsequent journeys in the mountains) my passport or diavatirio, as it were. For this superb bastouni was not only to excite the admiration – sometimes, indeed, the covetousness – of shepherds and others along the way; it was also to suggest, it seemed, through its link with the name of a family famous in Cretan history ('where did you get it?' was to become a regular question) that I was something more than a casual and external observer of the island and its people. Often, it was to be the bastouni that provided the point of entry into conversation, hospitality, and new friendships, and I continue to prize it for that reason, as well as for those occasions when it has saved me from violent contact with mountain rocks.

And so I seemed to be prepared, and Sunday 19th August arrived. Time to go.

CHAPTER TWO

Zakros to Analipsi:
the measure of the task

Kato Zakros is not quite the most easterly point of Crete. But whereas its site symbolises the island's rich history, Vai beach to the north, which protrudes a little further into the Mediterranean, represented for me the Crete that I wished to avoid as far as possible, with its coach-party and back-packer tawdriness. The choice of a starting-point, as I've said, had thus been an easy one. Even so, the beginning of the adventure was accompanied by a mild element of that 'reliable disorder', as the writer Kevin Andrews has termed it with regard to Greece in general, which – in retrospect, at least – can add to the country's charms for those content to move to its slower rhythms rather to their own, more insistent, northern or transatlantic ones.

My plan had been to catch a succession of buses from Elounda, through Ayios Nikolaos and Sitia, to Kato Zakros itself, there to launch the enterprise with a short late-afternoon stroll towards the south-eastern corner of the island. But the scheduled bus from Sitia was *hors de combat*, it seemed, and therefore there was nothing for it but to get off the Sitia-to-Vai service at Palekastro and begin to walk south from there, towards Kato Zakros about fifteen miles away. The first hour that ensued was to be probably the least enjoyable of the entire experience. I felt that in a sense I was walking without getting anywhere, while the unspectacular but remorselessly long hills on which I found myself soon made me aware that the 33 lbs or so on my back were going to take some getting used to on long hauls. To add

to my irritation, a fiercely gusting wind in my face repeatedly
blew the wide brim of my cricket sun-hat down across the bridge
of my nose, thus presenting me with the choice of either
accepting a field of vision that was restricted to the ground about
two paces ahead of my boots or of adopting a head-up, look-
down-the-nose posture suggestive of some manic drill-sergeant
in the Brigade of Guards.

I had settled for the former and humbler stance as more fitting
to the circumstances – in my mind, I had not even begun my
journey proper – when an elderly Cretan, bound for home in a
small village a few miles on, lifted my spirits by stopping,
unasked, to give me a lift in his pick-up truck. Moreover, having
pronounced my enterprise a splendid one, he then solved the
problem of onward transportation from his village in typically
Cretan fashion, by marching into the middle of the road and
simply holding up the first car that appeared. Fortunately, the
young French couple, who were indeed bound for Kato Zakros,
seemed happy enough to comply with my supporter's statement
that they were to convey me thither. Also, the need to switch
tongues to French – it was my new benefactors' first visit to the
island, and they had many questions – provided its own relief, if
at the same time another reminder of how much I needed still to
work at Greek conversation.

The French thread was to reappear twice more during the walk
that lay ahead, but on this occasion it was soon lost to view.
Instead of having to ease our way down the winding, dusty track
to Kato Zakros that I had followed on my first visit several years
earlier, we were able to speed along the new road that took us in
a series of broad sweeps from the heights to the water's edge and
to the Minoan site itself. There, to the slight bemusement still
of my hosts, I shouldered my pack beside the eastern sea, let the
bastouni begin striking the ground in its one-in-every-four-steps
rhythm, and started back up the very hill that we had just driven
down. A quarter to four in the afternoon, and I was off at last.

*

For some while, as the road twisted its way steeply upwards, I was able to keep in view that network of walls, pavements and courtyards that constitute the remains of Minoan Zakros. I had clambered around them in the past, aided by Stergios Spanakis' invaluable guide, and so the rule I'd adopted, of not stopping to explore such places of interest, was all the easier to abide by on this early occasion. The very location of a palace here, close by the beach, bears witness to the confidence of the island's Minoan rulers; but however exposed the site in military terms, its treasures from the distant past were discovered only as recently as 1959 thanks to the efforts of two Cretans with an interest in their country's history: Emmanuel Phygetakis, a rope-maker from Sitia, and Nikos Kavantonis, a fisherman and taverna-owner from Kato Zakros itself. On the spot where Dilys Powell and the great Pendlebury among others had, all unawares, browsed around before the Second World War, in 1960 the commune of Zakros cleared the site ready for digging to begin in the following year under the supervision of Dr Nicholas Platon, a former Director of the Archaeological Museum in Iraklion.

Zakros, it seems, while much smaller than Knossos, was a late Minoan city of great wealth, with its own artisans working such raw materials as ivory, gold, and copper, brought in from the East as part of a flourishing seaborne trade. When tragedy struck around 1,500 BC in the form of an earthquake, however, the palace itself was instantly destroyed, and the population of the region rapidly diminished thereafter.[1]

But the area around Zakros was not done with upheavals. Further earthquakes were experienced there in the nineteenth century and again in 1926, when the severe tremors lasted as long as four minutes. Violence of a man-made kind, too, was

---

[1] Faure, rejecting the widely repeated notion that Minoan Crete had a million or so inhabitants, believes that by the time of Homer the island may have contained no more than around 185,000 people. The first reliable population figure appears to be one of just over 270,000 in the last quarter of the sixteenth century. According to Pashley, that number still almost obtained on the eve of the War of Independence against the Turks in 1821, but had dwindled to 129,000 by 1834, following the ensuing exodus of natives to newly free Greece. A figure of 300,000 was reached in 1900, while the current population stands at around 500,000.

visited upon the region, now so tranquil in its remoteness and fertility. Thus in 1821, for example, at the beginning of the War of Independence, a mere seventy Cretan rebels captured eight hundred Turkish soldiers nearby and slaughtered them all – only to be betrayed thereafter by one of their fellow countrymen, a priest, and brought to their own deaths at Turkish hands.

When Captain Spratt, Director of the Royal Navy's Mediterranean Survey, studied Crete in the years following 1851, he found the locality of Zakros, when viewed from the sea, to possess 'a wild, forbidding aspect . . . from the nakedness of the cliffs and mountains above.' And when he went ashore he discovered, as I was to do the following day, that the road up and over those mountains from 'Katocampo' – now Xerokambos – was 'exceedingly rugged and steep'. Of course, when compared to the central mountain block that culminates in Ida/Psiloritis, or to the Diktian group around Lasithi, or, even more so, to the majestic White Mountains in the West, these eastern ranges are lesser creatures. But that they are, indeed, mountains, and that if one descends again to sea-level after climbing out from the coastal plain around Zakros there are two sets of them, not one, to be traversed at this end of the island (the second being made up of the Thripti/Orno groups) will be readily apparent to anyone who travels this way on foot.

In fact, around 90% of Crete's surface area is made up of mountainous regions, so that Edward Lear's aphorism about the whole island being mountain, quoted earlier, was indeed warranted. Stanley Moss, likewise, put ashore on the island in 1944 in order to take part in the kidnapping of the commander of the German garrison, found it to be 'one huge conglomeration of rocks'. 'We reached the top of one peak,' he recalled later, 'only to see a fresh skyline towering over us. . . .'

This profusion provides plenty of opportunity for differing reckonings to be made as to the number of separate mountain blocks involved. Faure, for example, like me, sees five main ones, but lumps together the 'Sitia' or eastern group, while adding in what he calls the 'Amari' range. But whichever way the catalogue should run, the best detailed description of the entire, complex network of peaks is to be found in Pendlebury's *The Archaeology of Crete*. 'These merciless mountains' Leigh Fermor has called them in their entirety, their limestone dark for the most part, but varying in kind and colour nonetheless, and softening as it descends into lower regions such as those around Knossos, Phaestos and Sitia.

Not surprisingly, Cretan history includes among its features the mining and working of metals: copper, zinc, silver, chrome, and even gold, both before and during the time of the Venetian occupation. And, again not surprisingly, the island's inhabitants have been left with only a severely limited amount of truly fertile soil on which to cultivate their crops. (Willetts reckons it amounts to about one-quarter of that 30% of the entire surface area which can be described as suitable for crops, orchard produce, and permanent grazing.) Certainly, however, the narrow strip of land around Zakros must be counted among these precious fertile regions, even though it may have looked forbidding to Spratt. In the 1970s the community of Ano Zakros alone, according to Faure, possessed 80,000 young olive trees which produced over 400 tons of oil every year, joining a yield of thirty tons of corn and 25,000 litres of wine.

Minoan Zakros, too, had been rich in olives (a perfectly preserved jar of them being uncovered in 1964, 3,400 years after they had been put into conserve), while it drew in imports from Egypt and Syria among other regions. Minoan Crete as a whole shipped out wine, and the island was continuing to do so in the fifteenth and sixteenth centuries, not least to England – a connection which prompted the appointment of the first English Consul to the island, at Candia (now Iraklion), in 1522. 'This Isle,' wrote William Lithgow, a Scot who spent a couple of months travelling in Crete in 1610, 'produceth the best *Malvasy*, *Muscadine*, and *Leaticke* wines that are in the whole Universe. It yieldeth Orenges, Lemmons, Mellons, Cytrous, Grenadiers, Adams Apples, Raisins, Olives, Dates, Honey, Sugar, *Uva di Ere volte*, and all other kindes of fruite in abundance.' Wheat and sugar were both exported. And while the excellent cheeses of the island appear to have been mainly kept for consumption at home, another visitor, the distinguished churchman Richard Pococke, found in 1739 that the Cretan export trade remained an extensive and varied one, including

> 'sending oyl of olives to France to make soap, and for working their cloths; they export also a small quantity of silk, wax and honey into the [Aegean] Archipelago, and wine to all parts of the Levant, which is very strong and cheap; . . . they export raisins, figs, and almonds to many parts: English ships sometimes carry oyl from Candia both to Hamburg and to London.'

Even these brief extracts from past records fail to cover the entire range of commodities in which Cretans traded, both during Minoan times and subsequently. For example, it was off this eastern end of the island that Spratt, nearly a century and a half ago, watched sponge-divers at work: young men of remarkable endurance and lung-capacity who would carry a flat stone weighing about 20 lbs to pull them down to depths of as much as thirty or even forty fathoms (one fathom is six feet) beneath the surface, the divers staying under for between one and two minutes at a time. As for timber, it would figure more prominently than sponges on any comprehensive list of exports, with Cretan cyprus at one time being used extensively in shipbuilding not only by the Venetians, but also all around the Mediterranean, as well as being prized in the Egypt of the Pharaohs for the making of coffins.

This exporting of the island's trees, together with ravages wrought by man and goat, has brought about what in Pendlebury's view is 'the main change in the character of Crete since antiquity': namely, deforestation. The land that Spratt found from the eastern sea to be naked and forbidding would almost certainly have appeared softer and greener in the days when Minoan Zakros was flourishing. Even as late as 1596, Fynes Moryson, Fellow of Peterhouse, Cambridge, reported after visiting the island that cedar and cyprus trees were to be found in abundance, 'whereof many sweet smelling Chests are made and carried into forraine parts.' The slopes of Ida, too – now harshly bare on the northern side, and only lightly sprinkled with wild oak on the southern one – were seen by Moryson to be richly adorned with cedar and cyprus. And in Minoan times, according to Willetts, 'the whole of Crete west of Ida may well have been covered with forest.'

Here, then, was one contrast with the past to muse upon as I left the metalled road and turned south along a dusty track towards Xerokambos. The very dust itself, puffing up around my boots with every step I took (the island had not known rain for eight months at the time), recalled another such contrast: for during Minoan times, according to Faure, the rainfall and humidity were significantly greater than they are nowadays, when the scarcity of water has become a problem for the island as a whole, and not simply for those who would traverse the mountains on foot. My own position at that moment, perched on Crete's eastern tip, brought to mind a third important change that had taken place in the geographical features of my surroundings. For the 'balance' of the entire slab of land, so to speak, had shifted since Roman times. At some moment in the sixth century, a huge upheaval in the earth's plates had 'tilted the whole island as if on a pivot', in Pendlebury's words, its western end being raised by as much as twenty-six feet in places (as measured by Spratt, for example, between Selino and Lissos in the south-west corner), whereas in the East, many sandy stretches of beach where ships had been wont to lay up swiftly disappeared beneath the waves.

Despite such topographical changes, however, there are links between the island's present and its distant past that remain in place and that are to be felt, above all, as one walks over its fierce terrain and mixes with its mountain people. 'The present day Cretan', argued Pendlebury in the 1930s

> 'has, indeed, much of the Minoan in him, for the Minoan stock, like the Egyptian, was evidently one which readily absorbed new elements. All over the island today you see the wasp waists . . . the slim

hips, the high square shoulders and the long legs. Many a village boy might be a direct descendant of the Cup Bearer [a fresco discovered at Knossos, the original now on display in the Archaeological Museum in Iraklion] or the Priest King [another fresco], and who can deny that he may be? Minoan, too, is the sense of style which your modern Cretan has above other Greeks. His very dress, the baggy breeches, the headcloth, the belt, can all be paralleled in Minoan times.[1].

Moreover, even if the great forests of the past have gone from the island, there remain the olive trees (Willetts estimates that there are something like thirteen million in Crete as a whole): rank upon rank of swaying green and silver, their senior members proudly presenting trunks that knot and gnarl like an old person's hands in a drawing by Dürer. Interspersed among the olives stand the more dour carobs, their runner-bean-like fruits awaiting the September harvesting when entire families descend upon them, long sticks at the ready for knocking down the pods. (These are nowadays sold for animal feed for the most part; but their saccharine content is also utilised in foodstuffs for human consumption, and it has been argued – by Spratt among others – that it was these carob pods, not the winged insect, that, as 'locusts', sustained John the Baptist in the wilderness. I do not care greatly for them myself; but I would readily resort to them if stranded on a mountainside without other rations, and I am sure that they would keep an itinerant preacher going for some while.)

And there are still the herbs: source of both food and medicine for villagers in the past; source of perfumes, which once were exported around the eastern Mediterranean; source, in the par-

---

[1] Faure adds the argument that the dynamism of the Minoans has remained a central characteristic of the Cretan people. This opinion will no doubt surprise those visitors who observe the village men who sit for hours inside or outside the coffee-houses (kafeneia), flicking their worry beads or koboloyia to and fro across the back of their hands. But certainly one encounters, even so, a good many Cretans who are dynamic, as Faure suggests.

ticular form of richly scented thyme, of the island's distinctive honey. 'The Mountains', recorded George Sandys after his visit to Crete in 1611, 'afford diversity of Physical Herbs: as Cistus (and that in great quantity) from whence they do gather their Ladanum, Halimus, that resisteth famine, and Dictamnus, so soveraign for wounds.' Dittany was once widely used – and still is in the mountain villages – to make a herbal tea that I find extremely refreshing. And during a long day's climbing it has become a habit of mine to keep in my pocket a handful of thyme and other sources of delightful scents, to be brought out and crushed between the fingers when the going gets hard.

There also remain from ancient times, as mentioned earlier, some of the island's main routes – this, despite the coming of the bulldozer and the construction (along the northern coast especially) of fast modern roads. The ways that are available to someone wanting, as I did, to climb out of the easternmost plain are still in essence those that presented themselves to the sturdy Spratt a century and a quarter ago: still having to zigzag wildly in order to traverse a succession of steep ravines; still seeming to the walker to present a series of climbs that far outweigh the sum of any intervening descents. Nor, as I have indicated, are the maps that are available to the modern walker much better than those which prompted Pendlebury to cry out 60 years ago against their 'woeful inaccuracy'.

For the moment, as I embarked upon this first, easternmost section of my journey, there were no problems on this account. But before long I would be echoing the archaeologist – while at the same time, I confess, rather enjoying the uncertainty of it all. For if there were certainty, it would not, for me, be Crete.

My later-afternoon walk along to Xerokambos was a warm one – I reckoned the temperature to be around 95°F – but pleasant and without incident. It is a largely empty stretch of the island, and even Xerokambos itself has not yet collected a sufficient mass of holiday apartments and tavernas to disturb the tranquillity.

By early evening, my bastouni and the name of its bestower having already become an object of attention, despite the distance from Zoniana, I was installed in the back room of one of the widely scattered houses that make up the village. After eating in a nearby taverna, I lay on my simple, iron-framed bed, fending off the droning, kamikaze-like swoops of hard-green-shelled vromouses beetles and glancing through the recent copy of the *Guardian* that I had picked up in Sitia while waiting for that uncooperative bus. A 'Commentary' by George Schwartz caught my attention. With the Gulf crisis gathering momentum, he was arguing that Western leaders, not least Mrs Thatcher, should mount a campaign to make their countries – indeed, their peoples' very way of life – less dependent on non-renewable sources of energy. 'We shall need a new civilisation', he urged somewhat apocalyptically, 'based on sustainability, freed from the myth of endless growth in a finite world. There will be no peace until we do'. Meanwhile, why not choose to travel on foot, by bicycle, or at least by efficient public transport, rather than by private car? With my boots and staff waiting for the dawn and my enjoyment of a lively private car far from my mind, I felt smugly in sympathy with such austere exhortations.

When I went outside to wash (cold water, of course, is all that is ever available in such lodgings), the stillness surrounding the remote shelf of land on which Xerokambos is perched was striking, the silence broken only by a few echoing shouts of late returners from the taverna that seemed to resonate from the wall of mountain behind the village. The sky was a vivid mass of stars. I felt excited and somehow very private; secret, even. I also had no hesitation in deciding to start first thing the following morning, long before the taverna-cum-restaurant would open to provide breakfast for members of the small tourist community that lived around the village. To have waited until nine o'clock in order to be served some regular morning meal would not only have meant wasting two or three cool hours in which to begin climbing out of the plain; it would have entailed holding on to the comforts and rhythms of the tourist. In anticipation of such a situation (and no one renting a village room in Crete should expect even a cup of coffee to be produced in the morning, though occasionally a local kafeneion will open with the dawn), I had with me a large chunk of Zoniana sheep's cheese, glucose tablets, nuts and raisins. With resources such as these, together with a salt tablet or two, one has ample fuel on which to begin the day's labours.

And so I was off at first light, on the ever-winding haul of the dirt road that led to Ziros on the other side of the mountain barrier, the steepness of the route akin to that similarly zigzag-ging metalled road at the other end of the island which the tourist coaches take when they leave Hora Sfakion and grind their way up to the plateau above. A stiff breeze, though annoying when it once again forced down the brim of my hat, helped keep me from overheating, while the sweatband that I wore under the hat itself kept my eyes from smarting. It took two and a half hours in all to reach the top, the eastern sea shimmering beneath me in the morning sun. Another half an hour and I had passed through the valley in which huddled the silent hamlet of Hame-toulo; then on, beneath the high plateau which I had traversed the previous year and which is crowned with a formidable array of radar and electronic-intelligence scanners – no doubt more active than ever at that particular time, as they sucked infor-mation out of the ether above Iraq and Kuwait for onward transmission to Washington. It was an unwelcome reminder of my other life as a student of international relations, and I was glad when I had passed on down into the large village of Ziros.

Ziros, which has around one thousand inhabitants, provided a rough loaf of bread, still hot from the oven, and a tap from which I could replace the already warmed water that was left in my bottles. Neither on this nor on my previous visit did I sense that it was a particularly friendly place, however. Cretan villages, even ones situated close by one another, can differ greatly in this respect, as the anthropologist Michael Herzfeld has noted after a less amateurish and impressionistic study than mine. Thus, for example, in the region of Ayios Nikolaos I find Kroustas always a particularly warm community to walk through, but Vrouhas not so different in size, distinctly less so.

Around Ziros, even though tucked away from the perils of the coast itself, the people of Crete have experienced their full share of violence over the centuries. It was in this village in June 1821, for instance, that the Turkish Janitsar of Sitia gathered together many of the Christians of the region and had them slaughtered. Captain Spratt, who lodged with a family for the night in nearby Handras, found that even forty years on there remained extensive evidence of the destruction that had been inflicted by the Turks (assisted, sometimes by their Islamicised Cretan subjects) on those who had dared to seek independence, with about one half of the houses in Handras itself still in ruins.

The extremely basic nature of the interiors that remained intact made a strong impression on Spratt. Yet he noted also a 'primitive contentment' among the inhabitants, adding, in his agreeable way and somewhat out of keeping with his mid-Victorian background, that a 'passion for cleanliness' could in any case easily become an irritation. The observant sailor also enjoyed watching the ritual of a Cretan village wedding while staying in Handras, even though he added the aside in his journal – on what evidence is not clear – that 'infidelity and divorce' seemed to be common in parts of the island. The day before the ceremony itself, local virgins would decorate the bride's room with loaves of wheaten bread and leaves of orange, lemon, and myrtle trees;

> 'and upon the pillow they put three crowns, formed of thorn, myrtle-, and orange-leaves, – all of which are significant: by the thorn is signified long life, and endurance under its cares; by the myrtle- and orange-leaves that the love of the bride and bridegroom may be as sweet and lasting as the evergreens, and by the loaves of bread, plenty and peace.'

I shall be giving an account at a later stage of the journey of my own enjoyment of wedding festivities in the present-day mountain villages. It is worth emphasising here, though, that their village of origin still remains the central point in the lives of many Cretans who have long since moved to the island's towns or even 'up above' to the mainland. Thus it is common at Easter for a narrow village street to be jammed with the cars of those who have returned for the occasion. Or again, I recently attended a christening in a small village where a sizeable proportion of those partaking in the good-fellowship and junketing – including the baby itself and its parents – had come back from Athens in order that the ceremony could take place in the family's place of origin.[1]

Meanwhile my way from Ziros led through Handras itself and on to Etia, through a fertile countryside adorned with trees and the occasional wind-driven water-pump. There was also the very Cretan addition of the rusting corpse of a local bus, one pair of its wheels removed, the body left to gasp its last, upside down in a field, like some helpless beetle. Such ancient, green-and-cream buses, which still ply some of the routes to the more remote villages, baggage piled on the roof, the owner-driver sitting in state behind his lace-embroidered windscreen and beneath solemn icons and good-luck charms, possess for me infinitely more attraction than their powerful modern brethren that work the island's main routes. In their death, and especially when upturned as in this case, they remind me of their yet more battered counterparts in India, though the latters' demise is likely to have occurred as the sudden result of an accident amid the anarchic traffic of Calcutta or Old Delhi, rather than coming at the end of years of dignified and low-geared toil to and from the mountain communities of Crete.

At Etia – where I had had to start jogging the year before – the handful of houses include one which serves as a reminder of life in the island before the arrival of the Turk: when it was the

---

[1] A Greek Orthodox christening – at least when conducted in such a village setting – is a more relaxed and convivial affair than its Anglican counterpart, with members of the audience (even perhaps the baby's father) wandering outside the church during the ceremony for a breath of fresh air or a chat with friends. The anointing of the infant's body in olive oil (particular attention appears to be paid to sexual organs) also has about it an earthiness that I find attractive.

Venetians who held intolerant sway, between the early thirteenth and mid-seventeenth centuries. For close by the road stand the (largely reconstructed) remains of a late-fifteenth century, three-storey Venetian villa: a villa which was once the home of the administrator of the region, and which in Spratt's words combined 'strength, luxury, and taste'. Much later, during the fighting of the 1820s, it had been used as a stronghold by the Turks, and had been considerably damaged when its occupants were forced to surrender by Cretan patriots in 1828. Further dilapidation occurred in 1897, when revolutionaries took materials from the fabric of the villa in order to construct a church in the local village. But the Cretan Archaeological Service has subsequently restored much of the house, its Venetian heraldry still proud over the main door, the long row of windows that adorn its upper floor gracefully surveying a surrounding landscape that for Crete is unusually soft and green.

This entire eastern end of the island – regarded by some who live in more westerly regions as scarcely belonging to the same country as their own more rugged terrain – has in fact played a notable part in Cretan history. It was here, for example, that many of the pre-Dorian inhabitants of the island, known as Eteokrites, took refuge when the new conquerors arrived some time after 1100 BC. Before this, the entire province of Sitia had formed one of the earliest centres of Minoan civilisation, with the port of Mohlos and the island of Psira, as well as Zakros and Gournia, subsequently yielding much archaeological treasure in this regard. (The succession of maps contained in Pendlebury's volume offers the speediest means by which to appreciate the gradual westward spread of the Minoans along the length of the island.)

The eastern region was always vulnerable, however, lacking as it did the vast mountain strongholds that were available for the Sfakiots and others in the West. Thus, for instance, in 1460 and again in 1471, not long before that proud Venetian villa was built at Etia, Turkish pirates swarmed in from the coast to destroy a total of sixteen villages – including that of Lithines, through which my route now took me as I swung south-west and began to descend towards the sea once more. At Lithines, too, a castle that had been built by the Venetians was destroyed in 1828 during the War of Independence. The Turks who had taken refuge within its walls apparently hastened their own destruction by pouring on to the fires started by the besieging Cretans what they took to be pitchers of water, but which turned out instead to be that fiery island spirit, raki or tsikoudia, and which duly ensured that the conflagrations became unmanageable. Fellow lovers of the drink are duly warned.

Lithines, in fact, had been my notional stopping point on this, my first full day's march. But I arrived there far too early to think of calling a halt, and in any case the way now led downhill, even if the metalled road that I was following for the time being began to evoke Spratt's description of its earlier, earthern state as 'tedious and long'. The monotony was of course broken from time to time: by large flocks of sheep and goats on the move, their mellow bells offsetting the harsh, insistent clamour of the cicadas; by the sight of families at work in the fields, harvesting their grapes and bringing them by panniered mule to be laid out on long nets, there to begin drying in the sun en route to becoming raisins; and by the sudden, brief appearance – too brief for me to be able to signal my presence from where I sat taking a drink under some trees above the road itself – of two friends from Ayios Nikolaos, Stavros Markakis and his singing conductor George, as they piloted their torpid and all-but-empty bus down below me, along the route from Sitia to Ierapetra.

The decision to press on, which foreshadowed the raising of my anticipated daily mileage throughout the walk as a whole, was all the easier to take in that I felt in excellent condition, despite heat that I guessed was now in the high nineties. I had earlier resolved to set aside the practice that it is usually wise to adopt on long treks, of drinking only sparingly until the end of the day in order to avoid bringing on an even greater thirst. Dehydration seemed to me to pose a greater potential threat in the circumstances, and I had therefore accepted the need to carry a greater weight of water in order to be able to drink almost at will, while replenishing or renewing my supplies at every opportunity. Moreover, the weight of my pack, which had slightly troubled me as I grumbled up those pre-starting-line hills from Palekastro, now seemed almost a natural attachment to my back. And so I pushed on, down the near-deserted road that shimmered in the heat, to rejoin the sea at Analipsi.

But yet . . . There was a 'but yet': truly, in my little world of distances and gradients and water-supplies, a gaoler to bring forth, if not the monstrous malefactor feared by Shakespeare's Cleopatra, at least a threat and a problem that was to hang over me for the remainder of the journey. But yet there were blisters.

I had greeted the first intimations that such penalties were being levied on my feet with a mixture of astonishment and something approaching indignation. Was it for this that I had covered all those toughening, trouble-free miles in training, broken in my admirable boots, applied all that careful surgical spirit? But the fault, of course, was my own. What I had not foreseen was the extent to which the considerable weight of my pack would combine with those other elements that, on their own, I had long coped with – the great heat and consequent swelling of the feet; the unyielding nature of the surfaces beneath my boots – to create strains for feet and boots alike.

It would be tedious to recall hereafter every occasion on which this problem forced itself upon my attention, or the measures that I adopted in response. But it would be to leave aside what became a major feature of the entire experience if I failed to recall that this was something that threatened for a time to bring my ambitions to nought, until I had found means of overcoming it.

My feet, then, were much in my thoughts as I gave these offending items, together with the rest of me, a salt-water bath by swimming off the beach where I had found a room for the night. In terms of distance I had done well enough, having covered about twenty-eight miles in ten hours, and that including the long haul up from Xerokambos. The machine seemed to be in good order; but were my feet going to prove inadequate to their task? I lay back in the water and cursed. Even the surrounding eddies of tourism, into which I had allowed myself to be drawn by coming back down to the sea here at Analipsi, were no more than a minor irritation by comparison with this over-riding question.

I swam back to the beach and went inside to wash my sweat-
and dust-stained clothes, then to lance, dress, and cover with a
protective layer of lambswool the blisters themselves. Finally, I
drifted off to sleep while worrying away at the kind of practical
questions that I imagine are placed in front of trainee chirop-
odists. It was not how I had expected to end my first full day.

CHAPTER THREE

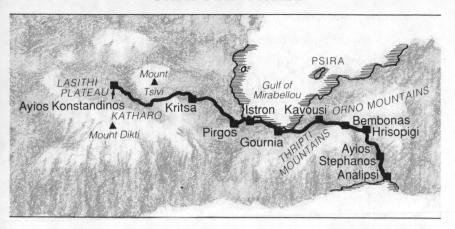

Analipsi to Ayios Konstandinos:
the heat of the day and the benefit of friends

My landlady, Maria (a considerable proportion of Cretan women bear that name), greeted me in her kitchen soon after dawn with a shriek of 'kalimera' (good morning), a cup of Greek coffee, and a bottle of water that she had turned to ice overnight in her freezer. She was a kind-hearted soul, fussing over her invalid husband, anxious over the prospect of an exceptionally hot day ahead and what it could mean for my crossing of the neighbouring mountains, and generally exuding briskness and good will in a voice whose timbre threatened to dismember the glasses on the surrounding shelves.

Promising (I fear with some inner reservations) to return another year in order to take a more leisurely holiday by the sea, I left her waving from her doorway. My route now turned roughly at right angles to the line of the previous day, switching to north with only a touch of west, in order to cross over the Orno and Thripti mountains to the opposite coast. This was a region that I had begun to explore, on its northern side, during the previous summer. Largely ignored in the guide-books, its mountains for the most part unsung, not a few of its hamlets, I had discovered, had been abandoned by their inhabitants: the doors of the empty houses padlocked, grapes mouldering on their vines, apple- and pear-trees bowed down or broken, even, by the weight of fruit left unpicked by owners who had gone off to towns that offered a less remote and exacting existence.

With the Libyan Sea soon gleaming below me in the sunrise, I climbed up the dirt-road that led from Analipsi to Ayios Stephanos, a village of pleasant appearance and about 700 people that stands 400 metres above sea level. The late Xan Fielding, a notable British agent in the island during the Second World War, has rightly observed that 'It is always a slight ordeal to enter a Cretan village unaccompanied by a local guide. After the gauntlet of brazen stares has been run, and the conventional words of greeting exchanged [the walker is always expected to open the conversation, not those seated], an uneasy silence falls. Then, suddenly, out of the blue, the leading question: "What are you doing here?"'

I was used to the ritual, of course, and to the ensuing litany of frank curiosity: Was I German? (Nearly always early on the list, possibly as a consequence of my colouring and upright stance.) How old was I? Did I have a family and where were they? And so on. And, of course, 'pou pas?': Where are you going? On this occasion, these and other questions were put to me by an elderly man who was riding out of the village on his mule in the same direction as myself, a couple of goats being tugged along behind. Adjusting my pace to that of the procession, I explained what I was attempting to do. '*All* of Crete? On *foot?*' The old man stopped the mule and I followed suit. He regarded me steadily for a moment, his face on the blacker side of brown from years spent working in the fields. Then he leaned over and down, and shook me fiercely by the hand. When we parted company soon afterwards, his way leading off the track into a grove of olive trees, I remained lifted by his generosity of spirit. 'These chance encounters on the road', as Fielding has written, 'are one of the joys of Crete. They never last long enough to allow the friendly curiosity of the people to become irksome. . . .'

My brief companion had also given me the benefit of detailed instructions as to which of the many turnings to take amid the network of twisting, dusty tracks that lay ahead. For this was the kind of area where, as Pendlebury had noted, the best available map was of little use. On the one I was carrying, a single unmetalled road was shown as linking Ayios Stephanos with Stavrohori and then Hrisopigi; on the ground, however, the choices of track were frequent and far from obvious. Indeed, on one occasion, despite the advice I had recently been given, it was only the further assistance of another elderly man, whose tethered mule I spotted under some trees about 400 yards off the track, that saved me from the consequences of a wrong decision that I had recently taken and that would have led me many miles out of my way. I also gratuitously complicated my own situation on another occasion, by opting to plunge straight down a terraced hillside of olive trees, steadied by my bastouni, in a bid to save myself the series of goose-necked bends by which the track was progressing – only to find when I emerged from the trees on to the dirt-road below that it was a different one altogether that had branched off from the original in the hidden fold of a neighbouring hill.

Even so, it was glorious walking at first, my way snaking up through quite dense bands of coniferous trees amid a deep silence and sense of solitude. Eventually I came to Hrisopigi, and there, opposite a stately line of eucalyptus that reminded me of my stays in Australia, joined the amiable group of locals who were seated on chairs outside the kafeneion. As before, the bastouni and the accompanying names of Zoniana and the Parasiris family seemed to render me eligible for an early seal of approval; but as was to happen on a good many occasions, it was the more immediate, known goals of the current day's walking that had more meaning and evoked more astonishment than did my targets in far-away parts of the island of which my interlocutors had no first-hand knowledge.

It was already the latter part of the morning. My water-bottles refilled, and safeguarded by these new acquaintances against missing a crucial, doubling-back turning above the village, I climbed on towards the highest point of the day's trek, beyond the hamlet of Bembonas. Now I saw and heard no one. Even the wind had dropped to a point where it ceased to stir whispers from the olive branches. Every step raised a cloud of dust, and dust coated the grasses and leaves at the side of the track. I had known it hotter in Crete, a few years earlier, when, during one phenomenal week that witnessed quite a number of deaths on the mainland from this cause, the temperature had reached 120°F in places. (On the first of the days in question, all unaware of what was coming, I had set out to climb up to the monastery of Faneromenis from the coast near Gournia, and although I had completed the walk, by its end I had usefully learned what dehydration felt like.) But certainly this present day was exceptionally hot, especially where I was climbing up, shut away in the valleys behind the Thripti Mountains without even the semblance of a breeze. Later, Vangelis Adamakis confirmed to me that even by the coast on the opposite side of the Gulf of Mirabellou, the thermometer had been registering over 100°F.

Eventually I drew near to where I expected Bembonas to appear; but although I could see a small chapel on a nearby hillside, and could hear the distant sounds of shepherds calling and whistling, no village came into view. Nor, looking ahead, could I see where the dirt-road I was following crossed over the ridge at the end of the valley, which now rose up like a wall about a mile in front of me. Finally, to complete the (far from atypical) puzzle, I rounded a bend to be confronted with a fork in the track with nothing to indicate which branch led to Kavousi, my point of aim on the northern coast, and which would merely exact a waste of effort by taking me far out of my way. I moved on for only fifty yards or so along the left-hand track, eased the pack off my back, and sought the shade of a tree. For the first – and it was to be the only – time on the walk, I felt not simply tiredness but an intimation that somewhere not too far off I could be demanding too much of my stamina. An intake of glucose and sheep's cheese seemed to be required.

I had just begun to carve into the comforting block of Zoniana cheese when, amid much rattling and a great cloud of dust, a battered pick-up truck ground its way up the track I had been following, took the other, right-hand fork, and headed for the ridge of mountain ahead. As it slowed, I shouted across to ask where Bembonas had got to, realising as I did so that among the half dozen or so cheery souls in the back of the truck was one of my earlier acquaintances from Hrisopigi. 'This way! This way! Come!' they yelled and beckoned back as the truck disappeared behind a screen of trees.

I duly followed, and found of course that there, in a dip behind that screen, stood the handful of houses that make up the hamlet of Bembonas. (The buildings themselves, like those in a great many Cretan villages, were unremarkable: single-storeyed concrete or stone, with a flat roof and metal-framed windows, the whole saved from downright ugliness only by a softening coat of whitewash.) Gratefully, I took my pack off once more and joined the truck-load of men and women, plus a couple of young shepherds, a few other adults and two or three children, in the shade outside the kafeneion.

The interlude that followed, though it lasted no more than fifty minutes or so, seemed to do more than either cheese or glucose could have done to restore my sense of possessing energy to spare. Thanks to the man from Hrisopigi, the nature of my enterprise was already known; but I still had to pass round the bastouni and my somewhat ferocious knife for inspection, and to tell of the riotous wedding celebrations, gunfire and all, which they knew took place in far-off mountain villages like Zoniana. None of the Bembonas group had been to those rugged regions beneath Psiloritis, and excessive compliments on my Greek were accompanied by an observation that appeared to be more valid: 'You know more of Crete than we do.'

Taken together with a rapid succession of glasses of raki, such generosity somehow helped make it seem unthinkable that my strength would prove inadequate to the day's demands, whatever the heat. Photographs of my daughters and granddaughter were passed around and suitably admired. And one of the local children, a girl of about three or four, constituted herself my special friend and helper, earnestly collecting up map-sections, bastouni and knife when they had done the rounds, and assisting me to refill my water-bottles from the spring that bubbled away nearby.

Solemnly, we exchanged names (hers was Marina), and I promised to return one day – a pledge that I hope to redeem in the near future. Then I loaded up once more, shook hands all round (the grip of the woman who ran the kafeneion was as powerful as the character that shone out of her face), and climbed up the steep track that I now could see wound its way from behind the village and over the ridge at the valley's end. At the summit I turned back for one last wave to the now miniature group below, raising my hat aloft on the bastouni. Then I passed through the wire-mesh gates across the track that kept sheep from straying out of the valley, and began the long descent towards the sea.

My vantage-point, high up on the divide between the northern and southern shores of the island, was a splendid one. But the intense heat was accompanied by a haze which meant that no more than the faint outlines of the Gulf of Mirabellou were to be seen from there that day. And so I went on down without further pause, to join a track that I had walked the year before, its dust lying thicker than any on the entire walk, the land on either side parched, for all that it was filled with trees and bushes. My shorts, hat, socks and scarlet running-vest darkened with a combination of sweat and dirt that no amount of scrubbing (I carried a nail-brush and washing liquid as a part of my mobile home) was able to remove completely, either that evening or thereafter.

Eventually I came down from the mountainside into the back streets of Kavousi, a delightful village which once boasted a factory that made perfume from herbs and whose quieter sections, away from the main coast road, provide splendid vistas which bring together flower-arched alleyways, whitewashed houses, and the soaring rock-face beyond. The village's terracing for vines rises to a height of 900 metres, up towards what I have already mentioned as a favourite, wind-swept perch of mine, the peak of Papoura. But alas, a track for cars has recently been bulldozed up to that eminence, while rumour has it that consideration is being given to the construction of a new airport on the low-lying neck of land below, beside the main road back to Ierapetra in the South and opposite the majestic Monastirakou gorge. The idea, it is said in the kafeneia, is to fly in a new breed of tourist by the jumbo-load from the East. Perhaps, as so often in Crete, talk and speculation is all the notion will amount to. I have to say that I hope so, for all that the people of the island need to safeguard their economic future. Otherwise I fear that the Crete I have come to love could find itself under further threat of being eclipsed.

Such misgivings were prompted by the final stage of the day's walk that now presented itself. Having drunk a good many litres of lemonade in one of Kavousi's shaded tavernas, I set off on what I had long anticipated would be the least enjoyable section of my route as a whole, along the island's main east–west road where it skirts the gulf of Mirabellou on its way to Ayios Nikolaos. Filthy from head to foot, and with my blisters beginning to make their presence felt as my feet became more swollen, I fear I was in no mood to feel other than a trifle testy as coach-loads and car-loads of tourists hammered past, or as swarms of young visitors on motorbikes buzzed within a few feet of my elbow. Many of these exuberant motorcyclists, I am sure, were far from possessing those qualities of the lager-lout that my dusty reflexes attributed to them; many of the faces that peered out from behind coach or car windows fronted minds, I don't doubt, that were genuinely curious about the island they were exploring, perhaps for the first time. But I had to work hard at forming such sensible and charitable responses, and longed all the while to be back up amid the silence of the mountains.

My plan had been to stop for the night at the camping site which stands beside the sea near where the track from the monastery of Faneromenis (of parched memory) joins the main road. But when I arrived there I felt that I still had some brisk walking in my legs, and there was the added consideration that it would be preferable if I could find a room, rather than a patch of camping ground, in which to readdress what I knew was the worsening problem of my blisters. So I carried on, past the remains of the Minoan town of Gournia that had been excavated by the American archaeologist Harriet Boyd early in the present century. Gournia, despite its possession of a small palace, had not been a rich town to rival Zakros or Knossos or Phaestos. Its inhabitants lived mainly by agriculture and such crafts as weaving and woodwork. Unfortified, and again completely open to attack from the sea, it was destroyed by fire and plunder shortly before the end of the Minoan period.

A few miles further on, and I was back amid a modern-day tourist settlement – in the corner of the bay close by the village of Kalo Horio, but again on the site of an ancient town: Istron. With its sandy beaches, this part of the northern coast has become a popular adjunct to Ayios Nikolaos, its concrete and bustle removing it by far from the scene which Spratt surveyed from his ship in the 1850s, when the Gulf of Mirabellou as a whole was

'enclosed by picturesque mountains on both sides . . . but presents no cultivation that is visible whilst sailing up the bay, not a single habitation on the shore; all looks wild and grand from the sea; Nature alone seems to reign around it, save and except the little speck of a fortress upon the islet of Spina Longa, near its entrance.'

Now, this beautiful region – once the Venetian province of Merabelo, centred upon a fortress that the Genoese had originally built in the town of Lato-to-Kamara, now Ayios Nikolaos – was rimmed with villas and hotels. But as far as a simple lodging-room went, Istron could present me with none that was free, however long I plodded up and down its length. If it had not been for the need to cope carefully with those damned blisters, the beach itself would have provided an adequate spot on which to rest up for the night, and I surveyed it with such a fall-back position in mind. (I was carrying with me a tough but light mat for such occasions, rolled up under my pack.) But I needed running water and an absence of grit of any kind. And so I talked myself into descending for a moment from the peaks of austerity and into a room in a small roadside hotel – the desk staff of which, the following morning, were spontaneously to halve my bill when they learned of the expedition on which I was embarked.

I must have presented an incongruous spectacle as I made my way across the lobby amid the somewhat genteel species of tourist that was murmuring and drifting around its carpeted seclusion: bastouni hooked over the top straps of my pack; hat liberally adorned with brown tide-marks of dust and sweat; once-white ankle-socks reduced almost to the same colour as my boots. But then, it had been twelve hours since I had left Analipsi and the Libyan Sea, during which time I had covered, as best I could reckon it, just over thirty miles across the mountains to span the island and reach the southern Aegean. If it had not been for the knowledge that something of a crisis had now to be faced over my growing number of blisters, I would have been pleased with myself.

After what seemed an age spent scouring my clothes, and after – the luxury of it! – showering myself in hot water, I crossed the road to one of Istron's numerous restaurants and did justice to a sizeable steak. Then I returned to my room and the matter of my feet. The left one had a blister on its ball which had not worsened much during the day; the right boasted a much longer specimen that ran across almost the entire width of the foot, just behind the toes, and which was a bit of a mess as the result of its dressing having shifted under the pounding. Both, I thought, could be contained at a level of discomfort that would not prevent my going on. More ominous, though, were the new swellings that had appeared on the outside of my left heel – fostered, no doubt, and their presence then made all the more noticeable, by my tendency to tread over to one side on the foot in question.

Rather than inflict upon the reader the tedium of repeated

references to this topic over the remainder of the journey, I will merely say now that it was indeed this outside of one heel that was to prove my most persistent problem, the resulting scars taking some months to heal completely after the trip was over. As it was, I did that night at Istron contemplate the possibility of being obliged to call a halt to proceedings. (A bus, caught at the very door of the hotel, would soon have had me on my way back to my apartment in Elounda.) 'I haven't had to slow [down] for [the blisters] all day,' I wrote in my journal that evening,

> '. . . but I have to ask the question how long I can go on subjecting [them] to such a load and so many kilometres a day. Gloomy. . . . Do I go on to . . . Katharo tomorrow, and take a fresh decision there? Or do I yield [to the discomfort] and trail home by bus from here? SHIT!! Will see how feet feel inside boots tomorrow a.m. I'm so loath to give up, when physically and mentally (feet apart) all is going so well.'

Even so, the decision to carry on and see how things went was present from the outset, I think, and I even came to derive a certain satisfaction from addressing myself to the task that was to occupy the best part of three-quarters of an hour each evening thereafter: lancing the new pockets of liquid; soaking the feet in cold water; applying antiseptic ointment, lint, and plaster-dressings; finally covering the offending area with lambswool, and pulling on a clean pair of cotton socks so that I could sleep with the dressings undisturbed. A second, thicker pair of cotton socks would then go on over the top in the morning, when the feet, back to their usual size, would easily slip into their boots. And it was not until several hours of renewed walking and heat had passed that discomfort, sometimes pain, began to force its way back to my attention.

And this, I decided as I lay in bed that night, was where the heart of the matter lay: it was a question of whether or not I was going to allow such discomforts to jeopardise a venture for which

I had prepared so carefully, and which in all other respects had begun so splendidly. The answer, of course, was clearly in the negative. And once that answer had been established in my mind, the entire problem assumed less threatening proportions. I would re-stock my dressings as soon as a pharmacy appeared along my route; I would remedy matters as far as possible each evening; and I would not be stopped by such an everyday inconvenience. That all but put an end to the matter, for all the evenings' curses that lay ahead, and it will require no more than the occasional, passing reference hereafter.

Thus it was with spirits restored that I left Istron early the next morning. My zest was all the greater in that I immediately left the main road and struck off inland, through the village of Pirgos, and plunged into yet another network of dusty tracks that snaked among the olives and the carobs, this time towards Kritsa and the foothills of my next mountain range, the Diktian. To my surprise, it took the best part of three hours to reach Kritsa itself. Again, the map showed a single, unmetalled road running from Pirgos; again, the reality on the ground was entirely different. And at one junction, so drastic and yet so ambigious was the choice before me that I simply sat in the shade and waited until there came along one Kostas from Pirgos, walking out to tend to his olive trees. Aged about sixty-five, he was not in good shape, his chest giving off great wheezing sounds as he went along. Nonetheless, he insisted not only on pointing out the branch of the track that I should follow, but also on climbing its first 400 rising and twisting yards with me in order to indicate further turnings that I would need to take over the next mile or so.

Even by nine o'clock the heat was beginning once more to rebound from the surrounding countryside. Back on familiar ground once my track had emerged onto the metalled road that came up from Ayios Nikolaos, I passed the three-aisled church of Panayia Kera, with its row of cyprus trees alongside, and with its famous fourteenth- and fifteenth-century frescoes – a vivid reminder of the importance of Crete as a preserver of Byzantium's heritage after the fall of Constantinople in 1453. I passed, too, on the outskirts of Kritsa, the turn-off that led to the beautiful site of the Dorian city of Lato, perched high above the fertile valley of Laconia.

And so into Kritsa itself, with its population of over 2,000; justifiably an attraction for tourists, with its winding streets and vine-covered alleyways. The importunings of the lace-makers, ever on the look-out for a customer, I could have done without. But I was glad to stop briefly in order to exchange greetings with the twinkly George Detorakis, who had made me an excellent pair of shepherd's boots some years before. (I recall how he had chuckled as he wrote down the measurements of my leg. When the winter becomes severe, even in sybaritic Sussex, I occasionally wear George's boots for warmth and comfort – though underneath, rather than in Cretan fashion over the top of, my trousers, not wishing to be seen lecturing on, say, the international politics of the 1930s looking like some elongated version of Mussolini.)

From Kritsa, as I have mentioned earlier, there are two routes by which to travel on foot up to the plateau of Lasithi, whither I was now bound. This time, in view of the load I was carrying, I had opted for the easier of the two: the dirt-road that winds steeply upwards to the West rather than the East of the peak of Katharo Tsivi (known also as Aloytha, and getting on for 5,000 feet in height). This had been a Minoan road in its time, and more recently in 1823 had been the route by which Turkish soldiers had climbed up to subdue rebellion in, and bring renewed destruction to, the Lasithi plateau itself. Now, the occasional farmer's truck would rattle up or down it, passing between Kritsa and the plain of Katharo. But for the most part, as I had come to know over the years, it lay silent amid the scrub and the herbs.

Again, there was scarcely a breath of wind, with the temperature, I imagine, somewhere around 100°F. It was with an inner smile, therefore, that I came upon an elderly shepherd (seventy-six years old, I was to learn) who was taking a rest under a tree from the same, broiling, uphill task as my own – and who was defiantly wearing, even so, two sweaters: a roll-neck one, with a second, V-necked companion over the top.[1] Manolis Koutoulakis lived in the Katharo plain during the summer, and was returning there after dealing with certain family matters back in Kritsa. His bearded face and balding head might have looked out from a canvas by Hogarth. His bastouni, much smaller and lighter than mine, tapped out a quicker rhythm as we fell into step alongside one another, while the loud squeak emitted by one of his well-worn boots as the weight rolled forward along its sole added its own syncopation. Indeed, in between bouts of conversation and pauses to shelter from the shimmering heat, I became quite hypnotised by the orchestrated noise that our joint passage over the ground was making: clonk (my bastouni); tap (his); squeak (the boot); and tap again: clonk tap squeak tap, remorselessly on.

Manolis was fine company. And although on the dirt-road itself I had to slow my pace to match his, my load notwithstanding, on those occasions when at his suggestion we cut across the neck of a loop in the track, traversing rock and scrub, he at once came into his goat-like own, and I suddenly had to work hard in order to keep up. (Spratt encountered the same agility in his sixty-year-old guide in the White Mountains, 'active and quick as the ibex [itself].') Like many shepherds, he had rubber patches fixed on to the soles of his boots to give him a better grip on the rocks (Spratt noted folded bands of untanned hide being used for the same purpose) – an advantage that was built into my own, lighter and shorter boots, designed and made back in Britain.

We stopped for a while under a wide and ancient olive tree, shade, until our arrival, for a large number of scrawny, somnolent sheep, its trunk grown to massive proportions. Nearby stood the mountain sheep-fold of a younger shepherd, Kostas, who soon strolled into view with his dogs, wrists looped over each end of the crook which lay horizontally across his shoulders, a pose that the island's shepherds frequently adopt and appear to find more restful than I do. Ice-cold water from his well was

---

[1] Sandy Rendel noted after his experiences in this area during the Second World War that one could come across a shepherd on a fiercely hot day on Mount Tsivi wearing a woollen sweater, while Xan Fielding, too, found that in far away Sfakia shepherds would wear a thick woollen vest under their shirt throughout the summer.

forthcoming; and then the three of us climbed on up the track to Kostas' main mountainside hut, where we sat for some time eating cheese and drinking raki.

Manolis, I think, had found the climb in the extreme heat a little trying, which was scarcely surprising given his age and the numerous layers of his garments. He decided that he would wait with Kostas until a vehicle came up the track, in which he could obtain a lift the rest of the way up to Katharo. And so after warm farewells I pushed on alone, stopping only once more before the summit in order to spread out in the sun my washing from the night before and in order to take a long, still look at the peak of Tsivi, opposite and above me, deciding that I must return and climb it before long

Apart from dominating the area between Dikti and the coast Tsivi possessed the added lure of having been the lair in the 1820s of the Cretan rebel leader, Manolis Kazanis, whose followers included for a time a young woman from Kritsa, Rodanthi, a bust of whom now stands in the village square. She had been seized by a Turk for his harem, had killed him, cut off her hair and put on man's clothing before climbing up to join Kazanis. Known to her companions as 'Spanomanolis', her true gender was discovered only when, in 1823, she was killed while fighting as one of the rebel band. During the Second World War, too, Tsivi had provided a refuge from and base against the oppressor, and it was here that Sandy Rendel worked with the partisans (andartes). On one occasion in March 1944, agreeable to recall, two German patrols searching for such trouble-makers ran into each other in the dark close to where I was now sitting, opening internecine fire at the cost of two dead and several wounded.[1]

---

[1] I went up to the top of Tsivi the following year, after climbing up from Kritsa to Katharo and spending the night outside Yannis Afordakos' kafeneion under as lovely a set of stars as I have ever seen – including the great displays of Australia's night skies. Festivities celebrating the patron-saint of the local church were under way in Katharo that evening, and as I lay awake into the small hours, track-suited against the cold, the sound of lira music echoed and re-echoed from the great wall of Mount Dikti on the far side of the plain. The climb up to the summit of Tsivi at dawn brought me a spectacular view of both the Gulf of Mirabellou and the Lasithi Plateau, together with a new shepherd friend, Michalis Kambanos, whom I had met once before in the hut of one of his relatives. As well as feeding me royally and proffering the usual steady supply of raki, Michalis showed me (I would never have found it otherwise the concealed entrance to the cave where Rendel and the partisans had hidden from the Germans.

I moved on, through the final belt of fir trees before beginning the gentle descent into the tranquil plain of Katharo which lies close up against the row of peaks culminating in Dikti itself. At a height of about 4,000 feet, the plain has to be left empty in the winter; but in the summer, when its inhabitants move back up from Krista, it provides fertile soil and good pasture as well as wonderfully fresh and stimulating air. (Its name, meaning 'clean', or 'clear', reflects this last characteristic.) As references to the neighbouring peak of Tsivi have suggested, anti-German activities flourished in this area, and it was into this plain, for example, that Patrick Leigh Fermor parachuted in February 1944 when on his way to set up and execute the capture of the island's German commander, General Kreipe.

Among the local andartes from those years was a friend, Yannis Afordakos. Stout-booted-and-breeched, lively eyed still, he has a small kafeneion at the entrance to the plain. To my disappointment, he was away (in Washington DC of all places, I later learned, where he had been staying with one of his children). A neighbouring kafeneion provided genial company, however, and insistent offerings of yet more raki, before I walked on between the fields of corn and fruit trees in order to reach, at the far end of the plain, the hut of a shepherd friend, Manolis Kambanos, before it grew dark.

Here, too, however, disappointment awaited me, for neither Manolis nor his wife was at home. As I sat carefully composing a note of greeting and regret in Greek, I had at the same time to fend off the attentions both of curious sheep and of their attendant dogs, the latter appearing to remember me from previous years and, far from doing their savage-guardian stuff, coming to lie across my feet in order to be stroked. I had first encountered this particular household when searching nearby for the narrow track which can take one, on foot only, out of Katharo, on to its western mountain rim, and thence down into Lasithi. Manolis (somewhat puzzled that I could not see what to him was an obvious line of advance) had helped guide me to the obscure beginning of the path in question – but only after he and his wife had insisted on feeding me. I had returned a few weeks later with a present of Scotch, and again in later years, on one occasion accompanied by my elder daughter. Her ability to climb that far and then to down her raki, along with the mutton, while seated by the hut's open fire had made no little impression on our hosts.[1]

I now had to summon up new energy to travel on in the fast-fading light, in order to find a bed for the night with other friends. The path up out of Katharo is clear enough once you have located its starting point, and is a fairly short one. But it has to be treated with respect, being extremely rocky and posing a constant threat to one's ankles as it follows a contour around a steep gully to emerge, with dramatic suddenness, on a crest above the Lasithi plateau, which lies below the level of Katharo itself. On this occasion, in the last of the day's light, I was glad to know the route well as I concentrated my attention on the loose rocks beneath my feet, with their familiar metallic chinking sound as they were dislodged by my boots or struck by the bastouni. At the summit I paused to take in probably the loveliest view of Lasithi I have ever enjoyed, the light soft and the shadows at their longest. Then it was a matter of intense concentration again, as I plunged down the steep face of small, loose rocks that led me through a belt of trees to the plain below.

And so across the fields of Lasithi – ampler and richer than those of Katharo – up the final, familiar slope at the rear of the village of Ayios Konstandinos, and into the welcoming oasis that always awaits me there after my treks in the region: the home (kafeneion and workshop as well) of my friends Stavros and Maria Philippaki. He is a teacher of mathematics at the secondary school in the nearby town of Tzermiadho, she a weaver and lace-maker extraordinary: a gentle dreamer who has travelled

[1] Faure, amid the scholarly exactitude of his substantial volume on Minoan Crete delivers himself of a splendid outburst on the subject of such hospitality: 'And who has not been bowled over by the moving hospitality of the shepherds and the countryfolk of Crete in their extremely humble dwellings, by the nobility and the dignity of their welcome, by their loyal friendship and their love?' Fielding, for his part, in his book *The Stronghold*, rightly adds that in return for such hospitality, the visitor is expected to provide news and conversation, to a degree that can on occasions become somewhat wearying.

outside Lasithi itself only infrequently, and outside the island only once, to Athens; but who journeys far beyond both in her mind. Their surprise was brief, their actions to ease the sweat- and dust-stained traveller prompt. A large tub of water was put on to heat up for the washing of both myself and my clothes. (Maria had to be firmly instructed that I, not she, would perform this latter chore.) A bed was prepared and an extra place laid at the family supper-table. Adults and children alike clustered around to tut and sigh over the blisters that, with relief, I could at last expose to air and cold water. Neighbours and kafeneion-gatherers – I knew many of them by sight – came in to chuckle over the size of my bastouni and the weight of my pack.

It had taken me around twelve hours to cover no more than about 24 miles, but then a fair portion of that time had been occupied, as I had always intended, by the enjoyment of the fellowship and hospitality of the mountains. I telephoned the Adamakis family, down in Elounda, to report progress. Then I slept well.

CHAPTER FOUR

Ayios Konstandinos to Kamares:
the pleasures of the unexpected

There can scarcely be a more beautiful or tranquil place in which to experience a Cretan dawn than the Lasithi plateau. From the terrace at the rear of the Philippakis' house the summit of Dikti shone forthright in the first rays of the sun, while all around, still cast in shade, the fields of the plain silently awaited the day's activity. Between the floor of the plateau and its surrounding peaks, streaks of mist hung horizontal and motionless in the still of first light. And as I left the comfort of my night's lodgings, for once fully breakfasted, the monks of the nearby Kroustalenia Monastery chanted their morning office, carried out and over the walls by loudspeakers, to hang with the mist and a scattering of early-rising butterflies on the limpid air.

The plateau, even at a lesser hour of day, had made a similar impact upon Spratt:

> 'The impression which the view of this deeply embosomed plain must recall to the traveller, on first beholding it, is that of the "Happy Valley" of Rasselas; for a wall of mountains completely encloses it, and, on all sides, access to it is gained only by winding rugged paths. It thus forms a perfect oasis amidst the stern sterile hills that embosom it; and, enjoying a tempered climate

more resembling that of Switzerland than of the populated parts of Crete in general, it is as salubrious as it is tranquil. . . .'

It is a tranquillity, however, that, both before and after Spratt's own visit, has been ferociously disturbed. The attractions that the Captain underlined brought human settlement to the area from Neolithic times, around 5,000 BC, as Pendlebury was able to demonstrate when in 1936 he began his excavations in the Trapeza cave just outside Tzermiadho. (The cave was also used for interments into the Minoan era, while Hellenistic and Byzantine artefacts were found there as well.) The importance of the plateau and its surrounding forts during the Minoan period is particularly well known, above all from that other cave at Psychro, at the opposite end of the plain. For it was here, as mythology has it, that Rhea, fleeing from the somewhat unsociable and paranoiac habits of her husband, Kronos (he had taken to swallowing his children lest they usurp his throne), gave birth to Zeus.[1]

Some would add that it was here, too, that Minos himself was born – the offspring of Zeus and of the fair Europa, whom the god, disguised as a bull, had plucked from the shores of Asia Minor. (The actual marriage of the couple is held to have been celebrated further westwards, at what was to be the Roman capital of Gortyn, and either in or under an evergreen tree – the latter always sounding to me the more comfortable nuptial position of the two.) Be that as it may, the Diktian cave at Psychro was a major place of worship and subsequently of archaeological treasure, although with the coming of the Dorians the Minoans had to flee to the surrounding mountains.

Two thousand or so years later, the burdens placed upon the people of Lasithi by an invader were heavy indeed. Following a succession of revolts in the region against their rule, the Venetians in 1263 drove all its inhabitants out of the plateau,

---

[1] The distinction to be made between the Zeus of Mount Olympus and Zeus Kretagenes – Cretan-born Zeus – is a matter for more expert pens than mine. For my part I am happy to note and accept the judgement of the Oxford scholar R. F. Willetts in his *Ancient Crete: A Social History* that the Cretan Zeus 'was like Dionysus in all essentials.'

destroyed their villages, tore up all their fruit trees, and forbade on pain of mutilation or death both further cultivation there and the grazing of cattle on the neighbouring mountain-slopes. The so-called civilised Venetians maintained this regime for the best part of two centuries, in the process wiping out virtually all traces of Lasithi's Byzantine heritage. The consequence is that none of the plateau's present villages dates back further than the fifteenth century, when an urgent need for grain and funds obliged the rulers of the Republic of Saint Mark to lease out cultivation rights on Lasithi, one-third of the resulting harvest having to go to Venice itself. It is widely held that it is from this period of resumed agricultural activity, and from the need to subdue the lake which the mountain-waters created after every winter, that there date the squares formed by irrigation ditches which are a notable feature of the plain to this day.[1]

The Turks in their turn were only a mite kinder to the people of Lasithi than their predecessors had been. Once again the plateau was a centre of resistance to alien rule. Once again, the penalty was destruction: in 1823, for example, as already mentioned (Pashley, on his visit in 1834, found one village to be inhabited solely by widows and young children); and again in May 1867, when a huge force of the Turkish regular army under Omer Pasha, having been conducted by a treacherous Cretan along an unguarded path beneath Mount Afendis on the plateau's western rim, fell upon the numerous but outnumbered rebel bands that had gathered here from around the island as a whole.

Nonetheless, Lasithi and its strong, gentle people survive. Its caves survive, exemplars of their importance – as places of worship, sanctuaries, sheepfolds – throughout Cretan history. (Faure, who is the leading student of the subject, estimates that there are around 3,000 caves in the entire island, at least one-half of them having been used as habitations at one time or another.) Even the region's mountain-top ceremonies survive, dating as

---

[1] Such is the explanation of no less an authority than Sterghios Spanakis in his *Crete: A Guide to Travel, History and Archaeology*. But Pendlebury argues in *The Archaeology of Crete* that the 'lines', as they are called, had their origins in Roman times.

they do back to around 2,000 BC, with Stavros Philippaki among others making an annual festive climb to the summit of Dikti.

Now my own route took me through the just-awakening town of Tzermiadho, past the road that climbs out towards Iraklion, and along a dirt track in the north-west corner of the plateau. At the roadside, just as I left the fields, a boy of about twelve or thirteen quietly stood guard over what I imagine were his family's sheep, grazing nearby. We greeted one another and I paused for a brief and solemn exchange. 'Are you a shepherd?' he asked, looking at my bastouni.

'No, but I have shepherd friends, and this is a present from them.'

'Are you going far?'

'To Psiloritis and Zoniana, where the bastouni came from, then on to Hania [that is, the province, not the town], if I can.'

'That is a long way.'

'Yes, but I must try.'

'Well, a good journey to you.'

'Many thanks. Perhaps we will meet again.'

My track wound its way up on to the mountain rim until – again, it was a sudden and breathtaking vista – I could look out far to the West and North-west: down to the coast between Iraklion and Hersonisos. The latter town, thronged with hordes of vacant-looking young tourists, is a focus for all that is cheap and raucous in what my Zoniona friends term 'non-Crete'. Yet once it was the harbour for the great Minoan city-state of Lyttos on the mountain-slopes above, its water aqueduct-supplied, its achievements embodying, in Spratt's words, 'great prosperity and advanced civilization.' The prosperity may still be considerable, of course.[1]

I had stopped to photograph this splendid panorama, to write up my notes, and to spread out my washing of the night before in the sun, when a shepherd suddenly appeared from the mountain-side nearby, a colourful sakkouli or woven bag slung across his back. The surprise was mutual. Hair and moustache

---

[1] Lyttos itself minted its own coins and rivalled Knossos in power for a time. Later, it sent a contingent of soldiers to fight alongside Idomeneus in the Trojan War.

thick and grizzled; brown eyes shining with intelligence, humour and contentment; baggy corduroy breeches tucked into tall black boots, Kostas Manousakis, it transpired, was exactly my own age of fifty-six. During the summer months his flocks were spread along this west-facing shelf of mountainside, while he himself lived in the village of Kastamonitsa, down below and a little to the South, where I was headed. I gathered up my washing – dry already after only twenty minutes or so[1] – closed my notebook and joined him on the track. We soon found that we had a friend in common in Zoniana, as well as other things less definable. When we paused in order to let him see to the water and feed at one of his flocks' gathering places, and I resumed my scribbling, he observed that the historian's rôle was of great importance – an attitude that I have quite often come across in the mountains of Crete, where learning of any kind is treated with a grave respect devoid of obsequiousness but far removed from the insecure and endemic philistinism of the English. (I carefully exempt the Scots, of course.)

After a while we came to Kostas' mitato or cheese-making hut on the mountain-side, with its supply of well-water nearby, its veranda shaded by the leaves of cut-down boughs, and its cool, dim interior redolent of competence and the smell of sheep's cheeses, some of which remained stored on the shelves that lined its walls. A couple of iron-framed beds stood in one corner; elsewhere, a rough table and battered chairs, a lamp, a breaker of water, jars of wine and of raki. A large bunch of grapes hung from a hook on the wall, alongside a bag of daki or dry-rusk bread, which is dipped in water and olive oil before being eaten. Empty sacks of sheep-feed were scattered around parts of the floor.

Kostas began to cut chunks off one of the cheeses with his bone-handled knife, his hands roughly dark and dexterous, his head and shoulders hunched intently over the task. Then we sat

---

[1] To avoid being encumbered with washing that had declined to dry in time, I had cunningly equipped the flap of my haversack with small loops from which, via clothes-pegs that had string attached to them, I could hang the damp items in question to dry as I walked along. In the event, and to the subsequent relief, I am sure, of those nearest and dearest to me, who would not have wished me to appear like a character out of Monty Python, this ingenious equipment was not needed.

at the table, stirring the bread in its bath of oil to make it palatable, passing the raki to and fro. We were joined by a more elderly shepherd who, delighted to learn that I was English, burst into reminiscences of the partisan activities in which he and Kostas' grandfather had participated during the war. ('Hospitable and charming' is how Rendel recollected Kastamonitsa in his memoirs, and it was chosen as the assembly-point in April 1944 for the party that went on to kidnap General Kreipe.) There was much talk of 'O Tom', Tom Dunbabin, Tasmanian, Fellow of All Souls and a greatly respected leader of the British behind-the-line parties on the island;[1] of 'Philadem', too, the name by which Leigh Fermor was commonly known among the islanders, from the title of a popular Cretan song that he was apparently wont to sing when in his peasant's disguise, not least in the presence of the German soldiery. I remarked in passing that I believed the great man now lived in the Peloponnese. 'Yes, but why?' came the fierce retort. 'He doesn't belong there! He belongs here with us in Crete!' (Even everyday opinions tend to be expressed by Cretans with an almost violent directness; when they grow heated, the volume can become quite intense.) With a certain inner relief I was able to say that I could throw no light on the matter.

Eventually the older shepherd departed, and I was thinking of following when Kostas announced simply: 'Now we will eat.' The cheese and so forth had been no more than mezethes, bits and pieces to accompany the raki. Now he produced in their place the canteen of hot food that he had brought up from the village with him that morning: chicken, potatoes and beans in a rich gravy. Coming as it did on top of Maria Philippaki's breakfast, it went far beyond my usual diet. But I fell to with enthusiasm, reluctantly drawing the line only when Kostas urged that I should rest in the hut during the afternoon heat, as he was about to do, and then, when he had further tended to his flocks, travel with him down to the village to spend the night there with his family. I felt that I had to maintain the momentum of my journey. But

---

[1] There is a vivid portrait of Dunbabin, as well as of Pendlebury and others, in Dilys Powell's lovely book, *The Villa Ariadne*.

I readily promised to return the following year. And when I had shouldered my pack once more and had turned at the first bend in the track to wave him goodbye, I sensed, as I think he did, that those couple of hours together on the mountain-side had seen the opening up of a friendship that would be a firm and lasting one. And so it has proved.

It was useful to have in my mind Kostas' advice that the dirt road, after snaking down for a couple more miles or so, would come to an abrupt end, and that my way would then lie down a steep gully to Kastamonitsa itself. In northern Europe we are accustomed to the notion that a road, once begun, must lead somewhere, to a town or at least a village; but in Crete, such routes will be bulldozed out of the side of a mountain simply to enable shepherds to get closer to their flocks by pick-up truck. Then, when the going becomes too precipitous, the bulldozer must stop, and the road with it. In this case, moreover, the way ahead from that point lay down a steeply plunging path that only my growing experience of the terrain enabled me to pick out amid the scrub and herbs. So acute, in fact, was the angle of descent that I was once more glad to have the bastouni to hand; and even this did not save me from sprawling headlong into a clump of agarthia, a herb which not only makes one sneeze a great deal, but whose dust is immensely irritating to the eyes. And so it was only after some delay, when I had eventually succeeded in washing the offending particles out from their lodging, that I entered Kastamonitsa,[1] stopping at the kafeneion for a lemonade and to have an accompanying raki pressed upon me by the owner.

There followed something of a trudge to the ancient market town of Arkalohori, across the wide plain that traverses the island from behind Iraklion. This region is rich in vines but otherwise not remarkable to the eye, although Spratt found its soil and rocks to be of considerable interest. A bus driver, his vehicle empty, stopped to offer me a free ride, then drove on, cheery but slightly puzzled over my preference for my own two feet. Not

---

[1] The name of Kastamonitsa is thought to have come from a town in Asia Minor, whence settlers were brought to Crete in 961 AD by Nikephorus Phocas, then a general and subsequently Emperor of Byzantium.

for the last time, an erroneous distance-figure on a sign-post – it was short by 50% – raised brief, false hopes that I would soon have respite from the heat and the nagging discomfort of the blisters.[1] But eventually Arkalohori did appear, a town of some size, complete with a Minoan cave in which sacrificial rites were once enacted, and a pharmacy where I restocked with plasters. (Without thinking, I turned around while inside the shop and with the pack that had become so much a part of me, caused havoc among displays of nail-varnish or some such item. The assistant smilingly forgave me, perhaps on the grounds of my valiant Greek, or of my rather fetching and gaily striped, if begrimed, sweat-band.)

The town, I learned, did boast one lodging-house for travellers. It formed the upper storey of a kafeneion-cum-bar, but as its owner was away for the day I was obliged to await his return, passing a couple of hours in the company of a set of friendly locals who vied with one another in keeping my glass and plate of mezethes filled. They seemed not to mind the declining standard of my Greek, and helped to take my mind off my rather swollen feet, which longed to be free of their imprisoning boots for the evening. (In just over ten hours, including the long and happy sojourn with Kostas Manousakis, I had covered another thirty miles or so.)

When eventually I was shown up to the single, large, upstairs room, which had about half a dozen metal bedsteads in it, I was glad to find that I was the only lodger for that night. Greek conversation could still be hard going for me at the end of a day's toil, and besides I appreciated having plenty of space in which to conduct the usual anti-blister operations. Toilet and cold-water washing facilities were available in an adjoining space under the slope of the roof, provided one could perform the contortions needed to enter and crouch there. Kneeling down, I scrubbed my increasingly disreputable-looking clothes as best I could, then ate well in a neighbouring taverna, and finally drifted off to sleep

[1] Stanley Moss wrote, following his 1944 visit to the island: 'Soon I came to learn that if a Cretan tells you a journey will take you so long, you are safe in doubling his estimate.' I concur, while adding, on the basis of evidence that goes far wider than the above episode alone, that sign-posts, too, may be greatly in error.

among the ranks of empty bedsteads whilst reflecting on the inner strength and mental alertness of the best of Cretan shepherds as I had come to know them.

Sleep was coming quickly enough each evening; but I was beginning to find that the sustained physical effort involved in the walk, together with my sense of exhilaration, was generating something within my system (endorphins, perhaps?) that stirred me to wake again after only a few hours of unconsciousness, and to itch to be off once more. I was also beginning to spend much of my half-waking hours in bed putting my thoughts into Greek, so important had such exercises become at various times during each day. In this context I was enjoying having to cope with the Cretan dialect, as well as with the complex language itself, and in deference to the former had long since adopted the softening of 'k' to 'ch', for example, in my own speech. I also found something satisfying about being able to declare, for instance, in a welcoming, questioning kafeneion, not the somewhat pompous-sounding English of 'I am a grandfather' but the forthright and rounded 'Papoos imai'. Such are the small pleasures that can cluster around ventures undertaken on one's own.

On first leaving Arkalohori soon after seven the next morning, I strayed from my intended route for a while. Having worked out the necessary correction, however, I eventually emerged on the dirt-road that I had been aiming for and that wound its undulating way westwards between the vines and the olive groves, on across the island's central plain. The small village of Panorama (the placing of the accent on the 'o' makes it a surprisingly difficult name for a native English-speaker to pronounce with ease) lay along the track, looking down, as I had anticipated, from its (modest) eminence on to the fertile surrounding land. A group of about a dozen men, women and children was already sitting out on chairs in the narrow street, and their welcome was a vigorous one. In no time I was seated among them, the already-warming water in my bottles had been replaced for me by the ice-cold variety, and (it was about ten-thirty in the morning) two large glassfuls of raki had been presented for my attention. My venture and what I had managed to achieve to date were cheered and toasted, and I was urged not to falter.[1] The usual personal questions were asked and answered, again to the accompaniment of a grave respect for the professing of history, and well-thumbed family photographs passed around once more.

Then I was off down the hill, to repeated calls of 'Good journey', pleasantly and partially drunk, I soon realised, from so much raki so early on a near-empty stomach. A few miles further on, therefore, where the dirt-road joined a metalled one that cut at right angles across its line, I stopped again, spread out my previous evening's washing to dry, and put my feet up in the shade of a small tree. A pick-up truck came down the track and pulled up beside me; its sole occupant got out, with little more than a cheery greeting handed me a fresh cucumber, then got in again and drove away. This is the life, I thought: to be agreeably tipsy and showered with agricultural produce on a hot summer's morning in the middle of nowhere. And then it happened.

Rain. After eight parched months, the island, or at least my present part of it, was once more feeling rain on its hard-baked surfaces. It was difficult to believe that it was happening at first, but when that initial shower had eased I walked on. It was still warm, though the wind was rising, and I remained in nothing more than running-vest and shorts. On, through villages where young boys with the liveliest, cheekiest faces imaginable (I recalled Pendlebury's argument about likely continuities from Minoan times) shot around corners at the wheel of a tractor or called out from the back of a farm-lorry – offering to exchange their light-weight bastouni for mine or, in one instance, wanting to know with a grin, 'Where are your sheep?' On, through Melidohori, described somewhat sourly by Spratt as 'a miserable Turkish village of about ten families' (though he became excited soon

---

[1] The spontaneity with which Cretans in the rural areas celebrate is splendid. It might best be described by the journalistic misprint that appeared (can it have been anywhere but in the *Guardian*?) at the time of a dispute between the train-drivers union and British Rail: flexible roistering.

afterwards when he thought, wrongly, that he had discovered
the site of the ancient Greek city of Arkadia on top of a neighbouring rise). On, over a switchback of low hills, until at Larani
I left the dirt surface and joined the metalled road that comes
up northwards from Phaestos, eventually to swing westwards
through Megali Vrisi and thence up to Ayia Varvara, one of the
highest towns in Crete at 18,000 feet and standing on a ridge
that divides the north of the island from the south.[1]

The climb up this new road was long and hard. The wind
strengthened in my face until its fiercer gusts were bringing me
to a standstill, and the rain now decided to fall in earnest. On
several occasions I was urged by passing farmers to accept a lift
in their trucks and, soaked through as I was, I must have appeared
quite barmy to each of these would-be-benefactors when I cheer-
ily declined their offer. Having come so far, however, and having
learned to live with those wretched blisters, I had no intention
of surrendering now to mere wind and rain.

Still, it was something of a slog to get up to Ayia Varvara.
And what seemed appropriate to recall about that town itself was
not such historical detail as the ravages inflicted upon it by the
Turks in the nineteenth century, but rather the Cretan proverb
(I take it from Stergios Spanakis) which declares: 'It is raining
in Ayia Varvara, and even God doesn't understand it.' But at
least, I thought, everyone whom I had asked had assured me that
in such a sizeable community I would readily find a room for the
night: a happy notion that was speedily dispelled once I had
inquired in a number of kafeneia and, having left my pack and
bastouni in one of those establishments, had walked up and down
the main- and back-streets in the same quest for a bed. (A group
of small boys, anxious to be helpful, was soon accompanying me.
'My grandfather has a room,' suggested one gravely, a statement
that turned out to be correct only in its literal sense, but not, as
the old gentleman apologetically explained, in terms of a place
that a passing stranger could rent.)

[1] At the northern end of Ayia Varvara stands the church of the Prophet Ilias,
which is said by some to be the centre of the island on both its east–west and its north
–south axes.

I returned to the kafeneion where I had left my pack, the rain still ruling out any notion of sleeping in the open air. I also quickly ruled out the well-meant suggestion from one of the locals that I should catch the last bus into Iraklion, fifteen or so miles away, spend the night there, and return the following morning to resume my walk. I was, though, quite tired by now, having taken just over eleven hours to cover about twenty-seven miles, so much had the wind and slope slowed me down over the day's final stages. And so it was with alacrity that I accepted the offer of a man who was clearly related to the elderly lady running the kafeneion, and whose small shop, with its part-earthen, part stone-flagged floor and its few boxes of tomatoes and such like, was divided from the kafeneion itself only by a plywood partition. 'You can sleep on the floor here if you like,' he said. 'My home is full of people. But at least here you will be dry.'

His daughter, who was closing up the shop with him, demurred: 'But Father, the Kirios [gentleman] can't sleep here!' Gratefully, I assured them both that I would indeed be happy to stay there.

'All right, then. But you must come and eat with us at home first.'

And so I was saved from having to pass a damp and uncomfortable night in a church porch or some such place by the generosity towards a total stranger of Stavros Anoyianakis. First, though, he had some crates of plucked chicken carcasses to deliver. So we piled into the cab of his pick-up truck: Stavros, myself, and one of what I gathered were his many children – a vigorous, cheerful two-year-old who perched in between us, thus enabling me to admire his hair that had been cropped to a stubble. We debated which of the two of us had the least, and I think he conceded victory to the balding Frank. Then, the corpses duly delivered in a neighbouring village, and a raki and coffee having been consumed there, we returned through the still-dense rain to Ayia Varvara and to a small house that was indeed straining at the seams with humanity: Stavros' wife, Marina, his mother and six children. (When I returned the following summer with flowers for Marina, it was to learn that she was soon to give birth to her seventh child.)

We ate from a huge dish of rice and mutton, amid a lively atmosphere. Stavros himself, a strong supporter of the socialist party, PASOK, was both ebullient and family-orientated. His eldest son, Nikos, aged about fifteen and greatly envious of my bastouni and knife, was an apprentice shepherd, already with a flock of his own to guard, the animals being shut up for the night in a pen alongside the house. But it was Marina who insisted that there could be no question of my returning to lie on my plastic mat on the floor of the shop. 'We will make room for you here,' she announced with finality. And somehow they did.

Woken by young Nikos leading his sheep out of the yard, I was off at seven, once again combining my thanks with assurances that I would return another year. Heavy clouds still swirled around the mountains that now lay high above me to the right as I headed west again, along the southern flank of the island's central range, with Psiloritis its culmination. The road at first led steeply downwards in a series of loops, then began a long steady haul back upwards towards Kamares, seventeen or eighteen miles away, where I planned to spend the coming night before going over the top of the mountain barrier the next day.

I was about a mile into the descent from Ayia Varvara when there was a call from high up on the hillside above me. It was Nikos, already standing watch over his grazing flock, with a younger brother to assist him.[1] His voice carried down easily in the quiet of the morning: 'Good journey. Come back next year.' I called back a greeting and renewed thanks, then settled into my stride, the bastouni thumping out its reassuring rhythm, my spirits once more lifted by the kindness of Cretans.

A little further on, though, and I was overtaken by the need to attend to a bodily function that I had foregone earlier in the

[1] It is a frequent experience suddenly to catch sight of a shepherd standing silently, gazing down at the slopes below. So must all alien occupiers of the island have found that native eyes were upon them everywhere, even when the surrounding countryside appeared at first sight to be empty and theirs to command.

Anoyianakis house, lest I should add to what was evidently an excess of demands upon the toilet there. I therefore found a steep grassy slope below the road that led down into some fields below, and perched myself on one of its narrow shelves. All went well until I sought to rise, when one of my feet slipped from under me. My legs, imprisoned in my lowered shorts, could do nothing to save me; and so, bare-arsed, I went rolling down the slope for forty feet or so until I ended up in some bushes at the bottom. No injury was sustained; no one, it seemed, had witnessed the spectacle, though there was a man working a few fields off. It was some time, however, before I could cease my own laughing, cover myself once more with grubby decency, and climb back up to recover my pack.

An episode devoid of all amusement lay ahead as the clouds continued to shroud the peaks close above me to my right. I came, as I knew I would, to the site, with its memorial, where the Germans had shot twenty-five local patriots in August 1944, in an attempt to discourage resistance in the region. This savagery of the German occupation was a feature of recent Cretan history that was to come back to my attention frequently during the days ahead, and I will revert to it hereafter. As it was, I passed on from this particular sadness to enjoy the early-morning vitality of the nearby village of Yeryeri, where preparations were under way for a wedding that evening (it was now Saturday), and to buy an excellent, newly baked loaf that I proceeded to eat as I walked along.

A more intimate liveliness awaited me at Zaros, a few miles on, in the bar of one Andreas, a fervent PASOK supporter whose clientele-cum-friends were soon complimenting me on my Greek as it rose on raki-oiled wings to new and daringly inaccurate heights of eloquence. One of the group seated around our table, his hair styled in a sweep of Saturday brilliantine and a small flower perched behind one ear, began to sing. Another decided that I ought to take a look at Andreas' collection of 'girlie' photographs, stored in a somewhat grubby album behind the bar. The name of the Parasiris family, evoked by the usual stream of questions, made an even greater impression in these parts, of course, close by Psiloritis. One listener, though, a man in his sixties I judged, somewhat frail and with one eyepiece of his glasses misted over entirely, was clearly turning something over in his mind throughout the noisy exchanges. 'How old did you say you were?' he asked eventually. I told him. 'Ah. I see. I could have done what you're doing at that age, but now it would be difficult.' Fond grins all round, though of course for my part I simply nodded agreement.

Zaros stands at 1,150 feet above sea-level. The road – metalled, but with scarcely a vehicle moving on it – now climbed higher still, close to the monastery of Vrondissi, famous for its defiance of the foreign oppressor over the centuries, then on to Kamares at 1,710 feet. The sun came out at last and though the wind continued to blow, always against me, it seemed, the resulting balance of temperature was a pleasant one. The occasional tethered donkey or mule stared at me with great soulful eyes, its wooden saddle-kit lying nearby, in wait for further labours. Great chorus-lines of olive trees dipped and swayed their silvered heads in the wind, to the accompaniment of a loud rushing sound, and I stopped to scribble down my delight at it all.

Even when covering longer and emptier sections of the journey than this one, I experienced little in the way of tedium. The practical problems attendant on the exercise – of how much water to take on board, for example, or of the state of boots and blisters, or of the need to reconcile distances with times and food and lodgings for the evening – preoccupied my mind for much of the time. At some moment each day, too, when I was sure that I was alone, I declaimed with much feeling the twenty-four German poems by Müller that provide the basis of Schubert's incomparable 'Winterreise' song-cycle, a cycle that I was committed to performing from memory a few weeks after my return to England.

Fremd bin ich eingezogen,
Fremd zieh'ich wieder aus.[1]

---

[1] A stranger I came here,
And a stranger once again I depart.

The work's opening lines seemed less applicable to my own state with almost every day that passed in Crete. Nor was there a great deal of Müller's ice and snow to be seen. But there were other passages that at times seemed more apposite: concerning dogs, for example (of which more later):

'Es bellen die Hunde, es rasseln die Ketten.'[1]

Or indeed concerning my own preference for striking off where possible along narrow tracks and mountain-sides where I was sure to be alone:

'Was vermeid' ich denn die Wege,
Wo die andern Wand'rer gehn. . . .'[2]

Eventually I came to Kamares: famous for its cave situated on the slopes of Psiloritis above, discovered by one of the villagers in 1890, and the repository of a number of fine Minoan vases that had probably been used in religious services. In more recent times the village had been burned to the ground by the Germans in 1944 for providing shelter and assistance for partisans – that theme again.

I felt in holiday mood. It was only two o'clock in the afternoon, and already I had completed my day's walking. Now, in the many-roomed lodging-house (calling itself a hotel) where rows of metal-framed beds stood ready to receive hikers, I could devote more time than usual to my laundry and to my feet. By now I was having to lance new blisters on the outside of that left heel every day, but had become accustomed to the inconvenience. I wrote in my journal:

---

[1] The dogs are barking, their chains are rattling.

[2] Why do I pass by the highways
That other travellers take. . . .

'Despite blisters – and the tiredness of the final three hours of [what has sometimes been] a twelve-hour-day's slog – it *has* been so invigorating, and such fun, and so rewarding in terms of people met. I'm surprised at my own stamina; also at my filthy state!'

The only other occupants of the building, who arrived by bus at the same moment I walked in, were a party of about fifteen girls from Luxembourg, aged sixteen to eighteen I would say, who had come up to do a spot of guided walking the next day. They had no Greek, the landlady no French, and so I translated between the two, feeling no end of a lad in the process. Similar sentiments were also indulged in, I fear, when, later, some of the Luxembourgeoises broke off from chattering like a flock of starlings in their own room, next door to mine, and came in, via our common balcony, to giggle over my line of washing, to widen their eyes at the knife and the bastouni that lay upon my bed, and to 'ooh la' at the somewhat damaged state of my boots, one of which was beginning to lose a part of its sole.

We gathered again downstairs for a somewhat fatty evening meal, served by what seemed to be the mother of the woman who ran the place. An elderly lady with a beautiful, serene face, she had something eternally youthful about her, a quality emphasised by the long pair of pigtails that lay down her back. When not bringing dishes, she sat and read aloud to herself from a local newspaper.

Meanwhile the chatterings of my fellow northern-Europeans grew so excited as to seem almost manic. (They used *vachement* a great deal, when wishing to give added emphasis to an adjective, which I thought had become rather passé, in France at least.) They were an extremely amiable bunch, but were not yet possessed of the stillness of womanhood; and the unremarkable quality of their features was emphasised when there came to the bar at one end of the large dining-room a local beauty on the arm of her man. (I imagine that the couple were on their way to the evening's wedding festivities that were soon to begin in the centre of the village. At all events, the man simply wanted to buy a packet of cigarettes.) She was very dark and very upright, with a mane of lustrous hair and finely shaped eyes and mouth. In short, she was magnificent, and she knew it, surveying the rest of us with a cool assurance.

Such a sight, I have to say, is not common in Crete in my experience; but I recalled that one such had evidently presented itself to Robert Pashley in 1834. The Fellow of Trinity's insights into the island's history remain extremely valuable, but his observations about people are of a dry kind, and the overall tone of the two volumes does not exactly prompt the speculation that the sap might have been rising within him. Then, suddenly:

> 'About one o'clock, on entering the straggling village of Kakotikhi, I was struck with an apparition of female beauty, as, when once seen, can never be forgotten. This Cretan maiden's features were certainly more heavenly than I had ever seen in any "mortal mixture of earth's mould."'

One can never tell. My own thoughts on this occasion included the wholly unprofessional reflection that in their respective appearances the Luxembourgeoises on the one hand and the Cretan on the other were mirroring the contrasting topographies of their homelands: the one with little to distinguish it from the surrounding tedium of the northern European plain, the other possibly unique in its combination of fierce challenge and tranquil enchantments[1]. The historian Jules Michelet, of course, in his *Tableau de la France*, is one who has sought to make such connections between landscape and character. And Xan Fielding, too, has had a go in a Cretan setting, in his book *The Stronghold*. But I would not give my own reflections on this occasion any higher status than that of

---

[1] Pashley, for example, writes of one village in its cliff-lined valley: 'It is one of the most sequestered and quiet spots imaginable . . . half buried in the thick grove of olive-trees, carobs and almonds in the midst of which it is situated. This is one of the many spots in Crete which, if one could but be surrounded by some of the ordinary comforts of European life, would be a delightful refuge from the tumult and anxieties of the world. . . .'

lazy, end-of-day musings, and I have no doubt that there are many fine-looking women to be encountered in Luxembourg.

Supper completed, I telephoned both back to my base in Elounda and ahead, across the mountains to Zoniana, to tell the Parasiris family (it was the effervescent Irini who answered) that I would be coming over the top the next day. Then, in anticipation of that hard day's climbing to come, I went early to bed, stifling a desire to go down to the village square where the wedding bells were already ringing out, to be followed soon afterwards by the first volleys of gunfire, reverberating in the still night air.

I had been inducted into the fun of these mountain-village weddings a few years before, when Kostas Parasiris' eldest daughter, Ariana, had married another shepherd who possessed the same name as his father-in-law.[1] Fifteen hundred of us had sat down to eat in the square in front of the church at Zoniana on that occasion, the air vibrant with the shouts and laughter of fiercely moustached, gleaming-eyed shepherds in their high boots, most of them dressed from head to foot in black. The firing of pistols, rifles, and even automatic weapons had begun as bride and groom made their approach to the church, continuing thereafter throughout the celebrations. Herzfeld, in his detailed study of life in one such village, emphasises in this regard the close relationship between the possession and use of weapons, which is strictly speaking illegal, and pride both in one's capacity for self-defence and in one's ability to defy the law. Fielding, for his part, writes of 'the pallikari complex': that is to say, that worship of Crete's fighters for freedom which is inculcated in the young, and which, he believes, fosters also a 'childish passion for noise'. Whatever the case, the repeated volleys, taken together with the flow of wine and raki, the swirling conversation *con brio*, and the stirring music of the lira, creates a highly exuberant atmosphere, both when the plates of rice and mutton are being passed round and, later, when the dancing gets under way.

[1] Such is the duplication of names in these villages that it is essential, for example when addressing letters, to be aware of the alternative name by which a man is known. Thus, my friend the Father of Ariana is 'Fragokostas', and one of my climbing companions, Michalis Parasiris, is 'Karkakis'.

As a guest at such festivities one learns to be prepared: for example, by wearing a shirt and trousers that can take any amount of melon-juice, as the pinkish liquid runs off the hands whilst the fruit is being sliced and eaten; by tucking a shepherd's knife into one's belt in advance, ready for slicing mutton off the bone; by making sure that one's balance and alertness are still adequate before letting fly with a pistol into the blue-black darkness of the night sky. (I try to recall the clipped tones of my gunnery instructor in the Navy as an extra safety-check.)

It was thus with no little difficulty that I remained in my spartan bed while the sounds of such junketings poured in through the open window. Most seductive of all – in retrospect, I think I might just as well have dressed and gone down to watch, so wide awake was I – was the haunting sound of the lira, soulful and wildly stirring by turns. This three-stringed instrument, about the size of a violin but with a deeper body, its bow held from underneath, is peculiar to Crete. Its practitioners, like my friend Yannis Dafermos, learn their art by following tradition, while having to possess far more than instrumental skills alone. For to be numbered among the players who command respect – their features displayed on posters scattered around the villages and towns, rather like the pictures of film stars in India – they must be poets, also: not only singing traditional lyrics to the lira's accompaniment, but also composing their own mandinades, fifteen-syllable rhyming couplets, that are appropriate to the occasion in question.[1]

And so, for all my virtuous intentions, in the event it was not until around two in the morning that I fell asleep. The occasional splutter of gunfire was still echoing from the neighbouring moun-

---

[1] The poetic traditions remain strong in rural Crete. There are still men in the mountains, for example, who are able to recite from memory the *Erotokritos*, a lengthy narrative poem from the Renaissance period by Kornaros. George Psychoundakis, for his part, recently honoured by the Greek Academy for his translation of *The Odyssey* into Cretan dialect, provides examples of his own unaccompanied poetry in his war-memoir, *The Cretan Runner*. As for the process of composition itself, that is followed, in regard to a Sfakiot bard's (highly imaginative) account of the capture of General Kreipe, by James A. Notopoulos, in his essay, 'The Genesis of an Oral Heroic Poem', *Greek, Roman, and Byzantine Studies*, 3, 1960.

tain. The voices of elderly men, arguing politics at a table in the street nearby, drifted in to me in snatches. An owl, perched somewhere nearby, commenced its series of short, plaintive hoots, which is all, it seems, that the Cretan version of the species can manage. (Lear was very taken with them during his visit to the island.) As I grew more dozy, it was easy, looking up at the window, to reverse the realities of space and matter: the white of the overhanging balcony from the floor above becoming the sky, the rich darkness of the sky itself becoming the building. I thought with excitement of the great bulk of Psiloritis, waiting for me nearby, and of the choices I would have to make once I was out there on its flanks. But eventually, even these anticipatings could keep me awake no longer.

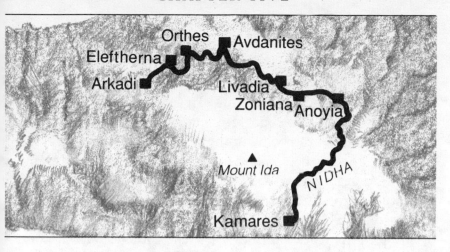

CHAPTER FIVE

Kamares to Arkadi:
the heart of the island

Looking back, I can see that I had become rather too pleased with myself, too confident that I would find the way ahead that I wanted. And I paid a small price for this state of mind the next morning, when I left the lodging-house at six-thirty, of necessity tiptoeing through a room full of sleeping Luxembourgeoises not yet braced for the exercise that lay ahead of them, their arms sprawled this way and that across their pillows.

I should have wandered the streets of Kamares the afternoon before in order to ascertain the exact route of my departure from the village for Psiloritis, but had been content, instead, to take my boots off and enjoy the sun. Now, following the wedding festivities that had come to an end only a few hours before, there was no one about to ask. I tried what looked a promising road, steep and narrow, running off the main street at right angles, towards the mountain. I had my maximum load of about 33 lbs in my pack, the water-bottles all full, and I was soon sweating profusely even at that cool hour. And then the way came to a dead end, at a large water-tank. There was nothing for it but to make my way down, feeling a trifle shamefaced, and to proceed

further along the road I had travelled the day before, back towards
the East, since I knew that it was on this side of the village that
I needed to begin my climb.

Fortunately, I found one elderly gentleman who was now up
and about, shuffling along in his carpet slippers to collect something from outside his door. He confirmed in rather vague terms
that I was indeed proceeding in the right direction, and so I passed
on beyond the village, looking up to the left for the line I wanted,
for I was determined not to follow the steady track along which
youthful visitors are taken upwards by local guides. At last, I
came across a shepherd loading materials and dogs into the back
of his pick-up truck outside his small cottage. Which way, I
asked, did he himself go up on to Psiloritis. 'Straight up there,'
he answered, pointing directly up the steep, rocky slope behind
his house, 'Past that line of trees.' (They stood on the skyline
above.) Then, with the directness that I had come to expect, and
after eyeing the size of my pack, he asked in turn: 'Do you think
you can do it?' I glanced up and, having never felt stronger, had
no hesitation in responding that I believed I could. A pause, while
he pondered, as if over the purchase of a mule, and: 'Yes, I think
you can.' Then, with a 'Good journey!' he was gone, and I turned
to begin the climb, as I did so switching my line of advance once
more through a right angle, across the end-to-end axis of the
island.

Many of the rocks that now came under my feet were loose,
but the bastouni never failed to do its job and I felt no temptation
to turn aside from my direct ascent in order to follow the path
that soon appeared, snaking more gently upwards. The sun began
to make its presence felt: less in terms of heat at this early hour
than of the deep shadows that now striped the smaller mountains
and outcrops behind and to either side of me. Soon afterwards,
the Libyan Sea came into view away to the South-west where
the island's coastline swings sharply southwards near Timbaki.
Up ahead, clusters of wild-oak trees were making this approach
to Psiloritis a far more attractive one than the bare rock-falls that
I had scaled the year before from the northern side with Michalis
and Kostas (the younger) Parasiris – they with their guns, ready

to blaze away at any game that should unwisely take to the air. Even so, it was as well that I knew (or thought I knew) what I was doing. For Dilys Powell's recollection of her own staunch, guided climb from this same southern side of the mountain, across the shoulder of Psiloritis to Anoyia on the other, should be heeded by anyone tempted to wander off on to this or any other of the island's major mountains unprepared:

> 'In this wilderness,' she reflects in *The Villa
> Ariadne*, '– arid, trackless – without a guide one
> would be irretrievably lost. . . . No water, no
> springs anywhere, only ridge upon ridge. . . . In
> front, I saw only the surge of the mountain like a
> sea of petrified waves.'

In fact, my own chosen route was eventually to provide a source of water, as I had hoped. I had climbed up, so far, on to the saddle above Kamares, which according to local legend marks the place where one of the island's giants, or sarandapihi – in fact, the greatest of them, one Digenes[1] – rode his horse on to the mountainside. Somewhere nearby – I did not propose to search for it – was the Kamares cave, while ahead the trees grew for a time more dense. Even so, the description recorded by William Lithgow in 1610 that the mountain was 'over-clad even to the top with *Cypre* trees' was now, alas, far from apposite.

The main, bare peak of Psiloritis itself stood above me, slightly to my left. (There are two, in fact, the slightly higher of them being crowned with a tiny chapel whose bell one rings on arrival.[2]) But I had already decided, before falling asleep the night before, that on this occasion I would content myself with a passage over its right shoulder, so to speak, and from there down into the plain of Nidha. The reason for making this reluctant choice lay not in the height or times involved – the view

---

[1] That is, of double, or mixed, parentage.

[2] The Church of the Holy Cross was built on the summit by a local priest after he had had a dream on the subject. I treasure an automatically taken photograph of Kostas, Michalis and myself, crouched beside it amid swirling clouds.

from the summit would have more than compensated for the additional effort – but in the state of my blisters and to a lesser extent that of my boots. I did not want further to jeopardise either item by having to place my feet at right angles to my line of descent on the loose rock-falls that sprawled downwards between the peak and Zoniana. My over-riding concern, I had argued to myself, must be to complete the walk in its entirety. And there would be other years in which to return to the summit of Psiloritis.

So I pressed on to the belt of trees ahead, having taken only two and a half hours to reach a shoulder where the ground, rather than forcing one ever upwards, began to fall away at last. Here, too, I found a spring and a watering place for the russet-coloured goats which were scattered throughout the trees around me, pouring the clear, cold water over my head and neck as well as refilling my bottles. I found also, daubed on the rocks at intervals of about twenty paces, dots of red paint that had been used to mark the way across the mountain, and for a while accepted them as my guide. They led me to a steepish drop, down into a gully, at the bottom of which I came across an empty shepherds' encampment where possessions of various kinds hung in sacks from the branches of trees, out of the reach of goats and other animals that might happen along. From here, I slowly climbed up the length of the gully itself, taking advantage as I did so of those pools of water, formed by the recent rain, that had been saved from evaporation by overhanging rocks. This haul brought me in its turn to the abrupt terminus of a bulldozed track; a track I could now follow, the walking brisk and easy once more, down into the plain of Nidha.

The sun was just lifting above the crest up to my right. And while I was unable to see the entire bodies of the animals in question, the backs of large numbers of sheep that were grazing somewhere between me and the skyline presented a ragged series of gleaming silhouettes as they were caught in the early-morning rays. Samuel Palmer might have done justice to the sight (certainly, my camera was unable to do so), though his own 'valley of vision', full of a much plumper species of sheep and of sifting moonlight amid the languors of early-nineteenth-century Kent, seemed distant indeed at that moment.

I had completed the really hard work of the day, and paused to watch excitedly as a pair of eagles circled quite low above me in the silence, their wide and jagged wing-tips stretched motionless in the currents of mountain air.[1] I have already recalled how Kazantzakis' Captain Michalis longed to be transformed into such a bird, so that he could look down from on high upon Crete in all its beauty. But perhaps the great and lamented Primo Levi was correct when he speculated that the dream so many of us have, of transcending gravity and soaring 'with the silent majesty of eagles and clouds,' is

> 'a forecast of an unspecified future in which the umbilical tearing away from the pull of Mother Earth will be gratuitous and obvious, and there will prevail a manner of locomotion much nobler than that on our two complicated, discontinuous legs, filled with internal frictions and at the same time in need of the external friction of the feet against the ground[2].'

Perhaps that is why so many of us, in the absence of the ideal, suffer those very frictions, internal and external, in order that our two complicated legs may at least propel us upwards to such sub-eagle vantage-points as Psiloritis or Katharo Tsivi?

---

[1] Rendel, in his *Appointment in Crete*, published in 1953, stated that there were no longer any eagles on the island. But I have no doubt that my silent companions that morning were indeed such birds. And in the following year, also, my partner and I were accompanied for a while by a similar, huge, jagged-winged bird as we crossed over the lower slopes of Psiloritis on its western side.

[2] From 'The Man Who Flies', in *The Mirror Maker* (trans. Raymond Rosenthal, London, 1990), a collection worthy to be classed in that European tradition of essays established by Montaigne.

My musings were broken into by the noisy arrival in their battered truck of two black-bearded, black-clad and thoroughly villainous-looking shepherds, who decided to enliven the morning by aiming their vehicle, complete with savage hound in the back, straight at me in a mock attack. As they pulled up a few inches short of their 'target', I responded by bringing my bastouni up to my shoulder and levelling it at their windscreen. Roars of laughter all round. 'Why are you carrying that knife?' they demanded. 'We're all friends here now. The war is over!' I explained that I found the knife most useful for cutting up my cheese, and – somewhat wearily, I fear – that in any case I was not German. This response, together with their inevitable discovery that I was a friend of the Parasiris family, led to the proposal that we should meet up that evening in a particular Zoniana kafeneion. But I knew, even as they charged off, the springs of their truck being hammered up and down by the rocky surface of the track, that they would not show up. It would have been most un-Cretan of them had they done so, for even appointments entered into with great solemnity are not thought of as socially binding in the rural parts of the island as they are in northern Europe and the United States, for example. Likewise, if one has invited, say, a couple of friends to supper at eight in the evening, it is essential to be prepared for the arrival instead of half a dozen people two hours later.

High jinks over, I could return to my thoughts about climbing, and about Ida/Psiloritis in particular. For the mountain from which I was now descending has exercised a fascination over human beings for thousands of years. Bound up with the worship of Zeus and of the Earth Mother Dimitra, its slopes have provided down the centuries a base for guerrillas and a refuge for women and children fleeing from the oppressor. In short, it has long been a symbol of the islanders' struggle to maintain their freedom. Some locals, too, hold that it was on this mountain, not on Dikti, that Zeus was born, as well as brought up, while Herzfeld notes that there remain villagers living beneath its peak who talk of the life of Zeus nearby 'as if it were a historical fact.' The Ideon cave, close beneath which I was now passing, was in any case accepted in Minoan times as where the god had been reared after being brought from that other cave underneath Dikti.[1] Newly discovered by a shepherd in 1884, it proved to be a rich repository of Minoan artefacts, some associated with the offering of sacrifices, for example, others with the celebration of the return of spring. According to legend, Minos himself came here at the beginning of every ninth year in order to ask his father, Zeus, face to face, for his approval and for guidance over law-making.

I have visited the cave on other occasions, and did not now pause to clamber up to its site on Nidha's western flank. I am not in any case greatly excited by caves of any kind. For me, rather, it was and remains the grandeur of the mountain above that is all: snow-capped until late spring, and even thereafter providing the climber with a well of pure, cold water on its very summit. Lear, on drawing it from a distance, described it as 'A dream-like vast pile of pale pink and lilac, with endless graduations and widths of distance. . . .', while the reactions of Spratt, when he had climbed it, were ones with which I could readily identify:

> 'Who can prevent the mind from soaring,' he asked afterwards, 'like an eagle that hovers over the summit he is upon, as he first beholds the diminutive and now silent, yet busy, world below, and thus feels the buoyant freedom of a temporary release from its vanities, intrigues, and bustle? Enthusiasm is, however, hardly the appropriate term for one's feelings on such an occasion; for it is mixed with awe and admiration, or with gratitude as the eye first reposes on the plunging descent beneath. . . .'

Spratt's own descent, like mine on this occasion, had been via the plain of Nidha, making his way through what he described

---

[1] Pendlebury associates the shift of religious focus from Dikti to Ida/Psiloritis with a shift in the locus of power within the island.

as a 'forest of ilex [wild oak] and maple' which then girdled the summit. Nidha itself stands at nearly 5,000 feet above sea level, and can be used for the grazing of flocks only from around May each year. The object of a struggle between rival villages in the later nineteenth century (it was the people of Anoyia who won), it has its own particular attractions which include a wild grass known as hrisohorto, or golden grass, so-called because its blades contain a phosphoric ingredient which leaves a golden sheen on the teeth of the sheep that eat it. When the Germans invaded in 1941, it was feared by Pendlebury that they might seek to land troops upon Nidha by glider, and a blocking party was duly despatched. Thereafter, the entire region became a centre of resistance. Tom Dunbabin, for example, had his headquarters in a cave on the mountain's southern slopes for some time, while a band of andartes under Petrakayeorgis also made Psiloritis its home. Perhaps best known of all wartime exploits in the island, the capture of General Kreipe was followed by the march of the successful band and their prisoner over the mountain, en route to a submarine journey to Egypt.

On his way up to the summit, Kreipe was taken through the large village of Anoyia, around fifteen or so winding miles below Nidha, and the place where I myself now came down from the mountain. It was not because of the Kreipe episode, however, but because of persistent attacks on their troops in the region (some provoked by the occupiers' attempts to recruit forced labour) that the Germans decided in August 1944 to burn to the ground this legendary home of fighting men[1], shooting forty-five people in the process. The village priest, Yannis Skoulas, had himself been a doughty member of the resistance, having gone to Egypt to train in parachuting among other things. When the Germans had finished their work that August, only his church and a couple of others were left standing.

---

[1] Spanakis writes of Anoyia in the first volume of his guide to Crete: 'Its inhabitants are different from other Cretans, even those of the closest villages in the same province [of Mylopotamos] as far as the mores and customs, social life, art and language are concerned. . . . Their hospitality is proverbial. . . .'

In all, the Germans destroyed about forty villages in Crete, quite aside from their wanton slaughter elsewhere. I was to come across further memorials to their handiwork along the walk ahead. Small wonder, then, that for all the islanders' traditional hospitality, together with the passing of time, one still encounters instances of a nurtured bitterness regarding those war years. In one village in Mylopotamos, for example, the province that I was now entering, I was to have stones thrown at me by a group of young boys (the range was too great for there to be any threat of damage) whose accompanying yells indicated that they assumed I was German. I understood the atavistic anger of my would-be assailants, which I suspect blended all too easily with the legacy of my own wartime childhood. Yet at the same time I felt a surge of sympathy for younger Germans (I have worked with a splendid succession of them at the University of Sussex) who, wholly innocent of wartime brutalities themselves, still have to live with such legacies from their forefathers.

The fact that my journey through the island was encompassing so many regions which had suffered at German hands in the not-so-distant past thus began to engender something of a knotted area within my own feelings, sentiments that were by no means wholly at one with my longtime self-identification as a European. And indeed the knots were to tighten with every site of German atrociousness through which I passed – until, as I shall relate, they were suddenly and unexpectedly eased at the very end of the venture.

Meanwhile, as I passed down the broad main street of Anoyia, I found myself caught up in a procession that formed part of the preliminaries to yet another wedding: the ritual in which relatives of the groom, having successfully 'plundered' the house of the bride, return in triumph with the gifts that her family are bestowing upon the marriage. It was a high-spirited occasion, with much laughter and joking that also involved the onlookers who thronged the street on either side. I felt something of an oddity in the midst of it all, but if I wished to keep moving then the procession was where I had to be. And so I carried on down the road with the celebrants, explaining to the amiably curious around me who I was and how I came to be there. (And for the umpteenth time – it began to sound rather pompous to my own ear – 'No, I'm not German; I'm English.') Eventually the path of the procession diverged from my own, and in sudden tranquillity I made my way down to the separate, lower part of the village, where I was called over to join for a while the taverna table of acquaintances whom I had passed earlier in the day, when they were picnicking from their car below Nidha.

I now had only four miles or so of road to cover before I reached Zoniana – a route along which the Turkish army had passed in the 1860s when bringing destruction to the region. I was already familiar with it, because at weekends the buses from Iraklion terminate at Anoyia, leaving me to walk this final stretch to my home-from-home. One last, steep rise and there was the village. I had taken eleven hours in all to cross over from Kamares, a distance very difficult to estimate given the zigzags one has to make on the mountain itself, but something around twenty-seven or twenty-eight miles in all. And here, by chance, at the entrance to the main street, was the Parasiris family pick-up truck, driven by Kostas' eldest son, Manolis. He waved excitedly, calling out to me to jump aboard; but to his amusement (and indeed to mine also), I declined – determined to walk even these last 400 yards or so down to the house rather than subsequently have to qualify in the slightest way the knowledge that I had walked the entire length of the island.

Zoniana, where life is perhaps conducted to a degree in the shade of Anoyia, has a population of around 1,500, and stands just under 2,000 feet above sea level. Until the 1960s, the great majority of the men of the village were engaged in work of a pastoral kind; but now, with the outside world (though not its tourism) increasingly penetrating the affairs of the community, shepherds make up less than a third of the adult male population. It is a society in change. But it remains the shepherds (not least, those of the Parasiris family in all its ramifications) who give the place its predominant character and tone. Like Cretan society as a whole, and indeed more so than in the island's urban areas, Zoniana could be described as a phallocracy.[1] This is not to say, of course, that the women of the village do not number among them many strong and forthright characters; but it is the males on whom the command, purpose, value and style of things are centred.

For anyone curious to know more of these values and life styles, there is the detailed anthropological study to which I have referred already: Michael Herzfeld's *The Poetics of Manhood. Contest and Identity in a Cretan Mountain Village.* (The actual village on which Herzfeld based his study is given by him the pseudonym of 'Glendi', and I will respect his considerate disguise. But it can be taken as being very similar in its essentials to Zoniana.) 'To the townsfolk,' writes Herzfeld, 'the Glendiots and their immediate neighbours are still fearsome mountain people, admired for their preservation of idealised ancient virtues as much as they are despised and feared for their supposed violence and lawlessness.' In return, the 'Glendiots', like the shepherds of Zoniana, tend to look down upon the lowlanders, and not least the people of eastern Crete, as a more effete species whose lives are wanting in the purity and independence which the safety, the traditions, and the very air of the mountain regions bestow upon those who are fortunate enough to live and work there.

On such matters as sheep-stealing and blood-feuds – matters of some fascination to lowlanders, in my experience, though both greatly reduced nowadays – Herzfeld offers ample guidance, as he does also on the life that centres upon the numerous kafeneia and on the traditions of hospitality that have made such an impact upon travellers down the centuries. Above all, Herzfeld to my mind has an excellent feel for his central subject: the 'poetics of manhood' in such a village, wherein 'there is less focus on "being a good man" than on "being *good at* being a man"'; wherein

[1] See, for example, the startled observations of Christa Wolf during her first visit to the island, recorded in her *Cassandra: A Novel and Four Essays* (trans. Jan Van Heurck, London, 1984).

what is prized is an ability to face the risks, dangers, and uncertainties of life with defiance and, not least, with style and ingenuity. Defiance of the elements, of a harsh fate, of authority; above all, of those who would curtail their freedom: such are the watchwords, for the most part axiomatic and unspoken, of the shepherds of villages like 'Glendi' and Zoniana. 'It is through risk,' concludes Herzfeld, 'that a Glendist shepherd discovers the meaning of his existence. . . . Life is regarded as a barren stretch of time, a blank page, on which the genuine poet of his own manhood must write as engaging an account as he can.'

Of course it is not difficult, in the world of the late twentieth century, to perceive anachronisms in all this. And the increasing intrusion of that world has brought problems, as well as enhanced wealth and comforts, to the people of a village like Zoniana. Indeed, Michael Smith, in his survey of Cretan history, has gone so far as to relate the underlying problem – one of identity and of purpose – to the people of the island as a whole. 'There is still no substitute,' he writes, 'for the purpose that is now dead – "Freedom or Death." Other societies, like our own, having grown used to materialism and tired of abstractions, have no need for a substitute. But a heroic society like the Cretan does need one.'

My own view is that the lowland parts of the island, and above all those that are thoroughly oriented towards the tourist trade, have already travelled a long way along the road that leads away from any need for heroics. But as regards villages like Zoniana, there is no doubt that Smith's observations have weight, even though the heroic tradition still remains much in evidence there. Of course, there is and no doubt always has been an element of the histrionic about the viewing of life in terms of the alternatives of 'Freedom or Death' – an outlook so vividly captured in Kazantzakis' novel of that name. The portraits of the male nineteenth-century resistance heroes that hang on the walls of the museum in the Arkadi monastery – there are courageous women, too, commemorated alongside them, and their collective act of defiance will be summarised below – are of individuals who are conscious of a need to cut a dash, from sariki (headband)[1], via moustache, to well-cut boots. But, as events at Arkadi in 1866 amply demonstrated, the style is an adornment to, not a substitute for, profound strength, reckless courage, and an unyielding adherence to the principle of freedom.

Thus, in my mind, the Cretans of the Arkadi/Anoyia/Zoniana tradition lie at one end of a spectrum among the people of my acquaintance, at the other being the likes of those among English 'liberal' academics whose fine principles are repeatedly and eloquently proclaimed, and whose essential invertebracy is glossed over with a sinuous skill that is wondrous to behold.

Zoniana lost seventeen of its menfolk at Arkadi in 1866, among them one of the leaders of that defiant action, George Parasiris. His bust now overlooks the church square: great-grandfather of Kostas' father, 'Boubouras',[2] at whose tiny kafeneion I now found Kostas himself (all leanness and attacking-eyed authority), his heavy-shouldered son-in-law of the same name, Michalis, and several others. Boubouras, too, was warm in his welcome, mumbling and twinkling away as ever from around his sweeping grey moustache; carrying his years as lightly as he does the seven wounds he received during the 1940 campaign in Albania against Mussolini's Italians.

I was spoiled, of course: with fortifying glasses of raki to begin with, and then, inside the Parasiris house, with food, a bowl of water for my feet, and a bed made ready so that I could have an immediate sleep (this was insisted upon) before we all sat down to supper. One of the children was despatched up the street to another of the family's houses, to return with a tube of superglue, thus enabling me to re-secure the sole that was threatening to peel away from one of my boots. The only item that was lacking in this shepherd's home was lambswool, which I wanted for use in blister-protection, my own supply having run out. But it was the wrong time of the year for such a commodity to be available,

---

[1] My own sariki, bestowed on me in Zoniana, is something I seldom wear, not wishing to be pretentious. But it came with me on the walk, in my pack.

[2] An affectionate nickname for one who mumbles.

and, indeed, the Cretan sheep, unlike its plump and comfortable counterpart on the South Downs of Sussex, provides such comforts from its back for very little of the time.

So I slept for a while in the main living-room of the house, with Anna Parasiris' wooden-framed loom on one side of it and a huge fridge full of sheep's cheeses on the other. Then supper, and fun with Kostas and Anna's granddaughter, just over a year old, who decided that she and I must imitate each other across the table, and at increasing speed, in pulling up our dress/running vest respectively in order to reveal all from the waist upwards.

Michalis Parasiris, one of my zestful companions on the summit of Psiloritis the year before and a shepherd in his early thirties, came in to look at my maps and to weigh my pack in his hand. He thought for a moment. 'I couldn't do it,' he concluded with typical generosity. I responded that I took that for a great compliment, but pointed down to where my blisters were being given some air before being dressed yet again (the outside of the left heel being by now something of a mess); then to myself as much as to him: 'I *must* finish.' Πρεπει να τελειωσω.

From above and below his exuberant moustache, Michalis grinned at me, shaking his head slightly as if pitying a hopeless case. 'Θα τελειωσεις,' he said with finality. 'You'll finish.'

I was up well before six the next morning to join Anna over a cup of coffee before she caught the bus down to Rethymnon and to her work in a hotel there. Her energy is phenomenal, with the daily arrangements of the household revolving around her and her attendant daughters. Her heart is similarly proportioned. Then, over the kitchen sink, I repeated the performance that so amuses the menfolk in particular: that is, my early-morning shave, which I had always insisted on completing even when we were setting off to climb before the dawn. (Zoniana shepherds tend to shave only once a week or so.) Kostas held up my steel mirror for me (it is an important safety item when on the mountains), chuckling even while accepting that I felt fresher for the exercise, and recalling once more the example set by a British soldier who had stayed in the village for a time during the war, and who had insisted on shaving even when German patrols were known to be approaching.

I promised the newly arrived Michalis that I would return the following year to join him and the younger Kostas on another 'safari' – the name that the two of them had given to a lively few hours that the three of us had spent the year before, with me at the wheel of the high-sprung four-wheeled-drive pick-up truck and the two of them standing in the back, guns at the ready, as we tore around the network of deserted, dusty tracks that lay between the village and the sheer face of Psiloritis, in search of partridges.[1] I embraced Anna, the children, and the menfolk alike. Then I set off down the street, pausing only to exchange greetings with Boubouras at the door of his kafeneion before climbing up out of the village and then beginning a long descent along the Rethymnon road.

Paul Faure tells us that the rock crystals that are to be found along the line of this particular road are of considerable interest, and in my ignorance I am ready to believe him. What I noticed at the time, rather, were the series of cheery greetings that came my way as I passed through the string of villages below Zoniana (the brief stone-throwing episode was a little way off), and the reverberations when I responded in Greek. To my thanks for being invited to stop for a coffee I would add the explanation that I had many kilometres to cover that day; then, as I passed on, I would hear the repeated phrases and comments bobbing around like so many corks in my wake: 'Did you hear what he said?'

---

[1] Immediately a bird or covey of birds took wing, Kostas would thump on the roof of the cab and cry out 'Stop!' in his best English. Almost simultaneously the guns would go off. My two passengers then leaped down, to go bounding over the rocks to ensure that birds which had been no more than wounded did not have time to hide themselves away. The victims' intestines would then be pulled out via the back passage with the use of a thorn twig, the carcass subsequently being lobbed into the cab to join the growing pile on the floor beside me. Truck, birds, and the three of us were soon covered in a thick film of reddish dust, raised by our dramatic succession of sprints and stops.

'He speaks Greek!' 'He said he had far to go.' 'He said he would try to come back next year.' And so on.

Already, before eight in the morning, groups of men were gathered in or outside the kafeneia, their voices echoing around the high, cool ceilings – cadences and volume sometimes shifting and rising to what in Britain would signal anger, in Crete merely a passing emphasis. The worry beads flicked back and forth across the back of hands, their owners' arms spread across the back of reversed wooden chairs. Monday or no, it was simply another day, and many of the older men would be content to while away its hours in this fashion, however active their youth might have been.

I went on through Livadia – briefly, in September 1860, the seat of the provisional government of free Cretans who had risen up against the Turk once again – through Kalivos and down as far as Avdanites before swinging sharply left on to a series of minor roads in order to cut at right angles across the island's east –west axis once again. The groves of trees were much thicker and more frequent now, although they provided little shade out on the road (sometimes metalled, more often dirt, always empty) as the temperature rose once more into the nineties. Again there was no breeze. In Orthes I stopped for a cheery session with locals in the kafeneion, while soon after I paused for rest and reflection opposite the ruins of Eleftherna: one of the most powerful cities in the island during the post-Minoan period, situated on a narrow sandstone promontory[1] and with huge water

---

[1] Spratt's description of the unusual terrain remains exact: 'The whole [area] represents a broad cake of white tertiary strata, which, having been uniformly elevated around the base of the mountain . . . has become divided into parallel but somewhat irregular strips by the mountain torrents, descending from time to time from the slopes of Ida, chaneling and cutting it into long ribbon-like ridges.' Eleftherna, being sited at the end of one such ridge, could be approached only by way of an extremely narrow neck of land that joined the ridge itself to the main body of the terrain. The Roman conqueror of Crete, Metellus, when attacking the city, is said to have had vinegar sprinkled on the stones of the main tower which guarded this entrance-point, in order to weaken them and thus enable a breach to be made. But treachery, rather, Spanakis suggests, might well have been the more prosaic cause of the Romans' success in seizing the city.

cisterns (one can walk in them now) cut deep into the soft rock that lies beneath the fortifications themselves.

And so, after ten hours and about thirty-five miles, I came to the supreme symbol of the Cretan spirit and Cretan independence: the monastery of Arkadi. The date of its initial founding is uncertain, while much of the handsome building that now stands in its huge surrounding courtyard – the doorway, for example – dates from the late nineteenth century only, being a replacement for sixteenth- and seventeenth-century construction that was destroyed during the violence which fell upon the place. We do know that as many as 300 monks were in residence around the turn of the seventeenth and eighteenth centuries, and that this number had dwindled to a mere twenty or so a hundred years later, when the monastery provided succour for those people in the area who rose up in rebellion against the Turks. In 1822, about fifty Turkish soldiers arrived to hunt for such troublemakers, fell asleep after drinking deeply from the monastery's celebrated cellar, and were killed by rebels summoned for the purpose by monks who had slipped out into the surrounding hills. During the Second World War, too, the tradition of resistance was maintained here, for which the Germans shot a number of the monks. And appropriately, in September 1944, it was at Arkadi that Dunbabin called together about ten of his fellow British agents from around the island, together with the leaders of the main bands of andartes (the abbot himself presiding over dinner), in order to coordinate moves against the Germans as the latter prepared to pull back into the area around Hania in the North-west.

But it is the Arkadi of November 1866, of course, briefly referred to earlier, that is commemorated to this day throughout not only Crete but Greece as a whole. On this occasion, following the proclamation of enosis (union with Greece) in Sfakia, several groups of the island's rebel fighters had gathered at the monastery, together with many women and children. A leader from the mainland, Panos Koroneos, joined them also, but, judging the place too vulnerable to an attack, moved out again to more remote regions, taking most of the andartes with him. The abbot and priests of the monastery, together with over 300 men under the leadership of Yannis Dimakopoulos from the Peloponnese and about 600 women and children, decided to stay, and were duly besieged by a Turkish army of about 15,000 men, complete with thirty cannon, commanded by Suliman Bey. The few members of the garrison who surrendered after assurances of good treatment were promptly butchered, and when the monastery's outbuildings had fallen (George Parasiris died there) and the Turks were pressing against the walls of the main building, those remaining inside took the decision to die in a manner that would also ensure the death of many of their foes. Who it was who actually fired the powder magazine remains a matter of debate – it may well have been Abbot Gabriel himself. In any event, just over 860 Cretans went to their deaths.

This dramatic sacrifice brought the Cretan cause to the forefront of European attention for a while at least. (Garibaldi, not surprisingly, paid eloquent tribute to the patriots, while British philhellenic societies subscribed to the purchase of a ship, renamed the *Arkadi*, which as I shall mention in a later chapter then began to run supplies to the island's remaining rebels.) This did not prevent the British Government, however, from continuing to manipulate the politics of the eastern Mediterranean in their own perceived interests and to the disadvantage of the Cretans, as they had done in the 1820s when passing the island over to the short-lived control of Mehemet Ali of Egypt. The supposedly supportive Russians, too, manoeuvred for what they saw as their own advantage, while the assistance provided for the rebels by the independent Greek Government in Athens was attenuated by factionalism.

Meanwhile the Government of the United States, for its part, broadly matched that of Britain in seeking to avoid giving offence to Turkey – much to the anger of the American Consul in Crete at this time, one William J. Stillman. Indeed, this forthright gentleman went into print thereafter, when he had left the island, to describe his own country's Minister in Athens as 'the most incapable, ignorant, and obsequious diplomat I have ever known in the service of our Government – a man who was an actual cipher in any political sense . . . [and] whose advent was, to use the words of one of the leading statesmen of Greece spoken to me at the time, "like a wet blanket" to the hopes of liberalism [in that country].'

What self-effacing junior diplomat; what time-serving member of middle-management; what academic, lowly or otherwise, obliged to work within a framework of bureaucratic incompetence and contempt, has not longed at times to speak out thus and be damned? Well, William J. Stillman did so (although it is true that he had already left his post), and I salute his sturdy, caring and undiplomatic soul across the century.

There were no rooms to be had anywhere in the immediate vicinity of Arkadi, and my intention was to inquire within the monastery itself in due course. (During a number of previous visits, I had come to know the gardener and the kindly, one-armed lady who looked after the church.) But my immediate priority, after so lengthy and hot a journey, was to eat well, and I duly repaired to the cafeteria-cum-restaurant that stands to one side of the monastery's forecourt, complete with a shop that sells tourist bric-a-brac.

It was the end of the day, though, and things were winding down. Moreover, the girl who was taking orders for food seemed completely thrown by being asked by a foreigner in Greek for a particular dish. She dawdled over other matters once she had produced the bottle of wine I had asked for, while her supervisor was taking no interest in proceedings, being busy parading himself (shirt well unbuttoned to reveal medallion on hairy chest) before friends who had come up to see him, no doubt from nearby Rethymnon. By the time I had reluctantly decided to remonstrate over the near-stasis that had descended upon my much-anticipated meal (I had eased off my boots, changed my socks, and written up my journal meanwhile), I was all but alone in the place. And by the time the food had ungraciously been put before me, the monastery itself had shut. So my bed would have to be under the sky.

Happily reconciled to such an outcome, and shrugging off the boorishness that had surrounded my meal (unique in the entire journey, but in a tourist location, naturally), I retained a sense of well-being that was reinforced by the wine. It then proceeded to rise to further heights as a group of black-clad shepherds, slightly incongruous in those surroundings, entered the restaurant and came over to my table in order to ask about my bastouni. It transpired that they were from Livadia, next door to Zoniana, the senior among them, Dimitris Niktaris, handsomely grizzled of hair and beard, explaining that each year they brought their large flock by slow stages to graze in the area around Arkadi. They had come down to the cafeteria for a drink from their encampment in the hills nearby, and naturally we were soon taking it in turns to buy rounds of the establishment's decidedly inferior raki.

With a bottle of wine already under my belt, I was thus pretty well drunk by the time I left my new friends in order to wash my socks before the cafeteria's toilets were locked against me. The prospect of having to pass a chilly night, up there in the foothills of Psiloritis, had become a yet more acceptable one, and it was simply a matter of slowly weaving my way around in order to find a suitable location. Meanwhile, as darkness fell, the shepherds departed, the cafeteria shut its doors, the surly staff drove off, and I was left happily alone in the huge forecourt.

The place to make my bed soon became obvious: on a ledge about two and a half feet off the ground; somewhere, moreover, that was tucked away and that possessed a small degree of shelter overhead. But the theatricality of it was such that I laughed and commented aloud to myself on how contrived my lodging was likely to appear in retrospect: for the ledge in question, with pine trees spreading above, formed part of the simple memorial arches that flanked the ossuary wherein lay the bones of the heroes of 1866. I hoped, I said, that no umbrage would be taken by the shades of George Parasiris and his companions. Indeed, far from any sacrilege being intended, it could be said that I was embarked upon a form of pilgrimage in celebration of the Cretan spirit that they themselves had so finely embodied.

There was no one else there to mind, besides the ghosts and myself, and so I unrolled my mat and prepared to make myself as comfortable as possible. After it had soon become apparent that the cold of the air was going to be even more of a problem than the hardness of the stone, I got unsteadily to my feet again and put on all the clothing, including a hooded tracksuit, that I was carrying with me. And although I was still to be woken by the cold from time to time, these extra layers, together with the wine and raki, were enough to drift me off into an initial unconsciousness.

As sleep drew near, I looked up at the silhouette of the pines against the sky, and at the stars beyond. The bells of a nearby herd of goats rippled and echoed with a pleasing musicality. One of those single-note owls (though alas, not one of the celebrated Cretan nightingales which had so captivated Lear among others) arrived to join in. Stone bed or no, life felt decidedly good.

CHAPTER SIX

Arkadi to Komitades:
more echoes of war

I woke for the last time at five-thirty a.m., and thus could enjoy the dawn that comes so suddenly during a Cretan summer. Shaving seemed out of the question for once, if I was to be on the move early, something I was especially keen to do since the day's journey would be along unfamiliar roads and tracks. As is always the case with raki, I find, no trace of a hangover from the previous evening's excesses with the Livadia shepherds clouded my head. As the light began to creep across the sky, I chewed a couple of handfuls of nuts, followed by a hunk of cheese and a salt-tablet. Then I was on my way again, by the road that leads into the foothills to the South of the monastery, past a scattering of fields and a grove of trees that were unusually large and handsome for Crete.

The map once again proved misleading at this stage, and I had climbed a long hill for a mile or so before, already uneasy at my direction, I called over to a shepherd who was standing on a nearby rise and was sent back down again – this time to branch off on the bulldozed, dirt-track that led to Thronos. (By now, such additional miles seemed neither here nor there, even though the sole of one of my boots was again giving cause for concern.) There followed a series of swoops as I crossed over those ridges, spread like so many gripping fingers, by which the great head and shoulders of Psiloritis, high on my left now, are bound into the main body of the island. In some ways, it was one of the bleaker stretches of my route; but again it was of historical interest, for it was along this way that the andartes had come by night in 1822 to kill the Turkish posse as it sprawled asleep in its cups in Arkadi below. I saw no one, however, not even ghosts.

Eventually the track began to wind its way down, carrying me with it into much softer country, dense with olives and other trees, the land continuing to shelve away towards the distant southern shore. I had reached Thronos, still 1,600 feet up: now an unimposing scattering of houses, but once the city of Sybrita and the seat of a bishopric (hence its present name). The outlines of its cathedral can still be traced around the remains of the eleventh-century Byzantine church that is itself richly adorned within, while being framed from the outside by the majesty of Psiloritis away to the North-east. When Spratt passed this way, the village of Thronos itself had been taken over by Turkish families. 'A finer site for a city I have not as yet seen,' he wrote, adding that so salubrious was the air that the alien residents claimed to have been entirely free of headaches since their arrival there.

I now stood on the edge of 'lotus land', as it was called by British agents in the island during the war: at the head of the Amari valley, arguably the loveliest spot in all of Crete, its village squares gushing water from the mountains behind, its fields heavy with fruit trees, corn, and olives. The harsh rock faces of Psiloritis, so near across the ground, seemed a world away.

The region contains about forty villages in all, with a total population of between 8 and 9,000 people. Its designation is taken from the village of Amari itself, a name perhaps derived from that of a Venetian family who once lived there. During the Second World War, behind-the-lines agents would come to the valley in order to exchange news and make plans, meeting amidst a local populace that, in the tradition of centuries, was resolutely opposed to the new barbarian oppressors and immensely hospitable to its friends and allies. (Tom Dunbabin, especially, was loved and admired throughout the valley.) In August 1944, as an act of pre-emptive terror aimed at discouraging any harassing of their coming withdrawal to the North-west coast of the island, the Germans destroyed nine villages here and shot 104 people in the process, forty-three of them in Yerakari alone.

Soon after passing through Thronos, and before turning down towards Yerakari, I was surprised to come across a roadside pharmacy where I could purchase a fresh stock of dressings for my feet from its enthusiastically welcoming owner. And on the opposite side of the road there stood a 'supermarket', no less. The two shops and a few houses seemed strangely isolated, there on the hillside. Conscious of the previous night's mild privations, I stocked up with orange-juice, fruit, and chocolate, then devoured almost the entire lot five minutes later as I sprawled in the sun in a field below the road.

The village of Meronas, which followed, was briefly the seat of a Turk-defying General Assembly of Crete in 1878. It seemed a warm and welcoming place, especially when I met there Ilias Vamiadakis, a young Australian-Cretan who returned to the island from Sydney for a few months every other year in order to look after the property that his family had left behind in Meronas when it emigrated. Trained as an accountant, Ilias had now sensibly switched to earning his living as a double-bass player, and I promised to look him up, and to listen to him perform, the next time I was in Sydney. We were joined by an uncle of his, who had taken food to British soldiers in hiding nearby after the defeat of 1941, and who recalled with much laughter how, three years later, the Germans had scoured the valley in vain for their abducted Commander. (Kreipe, Moss and Co. had actually been hiding for a time in a sheepfold above Yerakari – this, three months before that village was levelled to the ground. Making fools of the Master Race was, for Cretans, almost as agreeable as killing them.)

I soon came to Yerakari itself, further down the valley, where a severe defeat had been inflicted upon the Ṭurks during the uprising of 1866–68. A group of women, chatting in front of their new (post-war) houses, insisted that I stop for a beautifully refreshing glass of kanellada, made from cinnamon, while a short way on a group of men, sitting at a table outside a kafeneion, followed suit with mezethes and my first raki of the day.

To my regret, however, my way now lay out of the Amari valley. I swung off to the West – even North-west at first – in order to climb over a spur of Mount Kedros and to snake around two sides of a triangle while by-passing the worst of that sharp eminence, before dropping down again into Spili. After the met-alled road of the valley, it was a dusty, silent track that I was now following: silent, that is, save for the clear, strong singing of an elderly man, straw-hatted, his face dark with years of the sun, who, without realising I was there, passed me by as I stopped for water under a clump of trees; one mule beneath his swaying body, another, led by a long strap, piled high with the fruits of his fields and his labours.

This was to be one of my shorter days of walking, for by four in the afternoon, with only just over twenty-five miles com-pleted, I was plunging down to the delightful small town of Spili. Nestling close under the mountain-side, its twisting, narrow backstreets filling the eye with low, tiled roofs and sudden bal-conies, with vines, flowers, and mysterious side-passages, Spili quite rightly attracts a passing tourist trade. Greeks, too, had come there to take the waters that gush out of a long row of ornate orifices in the small, trim, tree-shaded square. This far was enough for the day, I decided, not least in my dust-covered and unshaven state. Besides, I had in my notebook the name of a friend of Vangelis Adamakis whom I had promised to look up, a man who had served in the army with Vangelis, and who now was clerk of the local court here – Yannis Astrinakis.

I therefore obtained a room for the night – complete with the luxury of a shower – despite the temporary absence of its owner and through the good offices of the lively, spring-heeled George Afteyakis, whose kafeneion stood opposite. With time to spare, and with the rare advantage of hot water on tap, I could once again seek to scrub the worst of the reddy-brown dust out of my clothes. I could linger over the growing inconvenience of my left heel and over the problem of how to ensure that my boots, too, lasted the course, for contrary to my initial estimates they had already been subjected to a pounding of over 250 miles. Indeed, my journal for the day serves as a reminder that occasionally I could still entertain the thought that I might be forced to call a halt to the enterprise:

> 'Hope my joints – and above all my feet – can keep
> it up to the end. The total [mileage] is likely to be
> astonishingly high. If only there were no pain in
> [my] feet I'd have no doubt.'

My chores completed, I climbed the set of concrete stairs that led from my balcony to the roof of the building in order to enjoy the leafy vistas across neighbouring tiles to the mountain-side close beyond. Then, as the evening opened, I crossed the street to the Afteyakis kafeneion, where groups of animated locals were already busy at their tables playing cards or draughts. I found that George himself had spread the word of what I was up to, and at once there arrived at my own table the first of what was to be a series of drinks, together with potatoes cooked in their jackets, olives, and other mezethes, bought for me by men who remained no more than a smiling face or an arm uplifted in greeting in some distant corner of the noisy, smoky, laughter-filled room. Yannis Astrinakis arrived, too, having been sent for by George: a little hesitant and even shy at first (he had had no forewarning from Vangelis of my possible appearance in the town), but warm and relaxed as the evening progressed. He seemed to enjoy my quip that I would be completing the trip, not on foot (meh ta pothia), so much as on blisters (meh ta fouskales).

Spili – its name derived from a small cave nearby – has its own place in the history of the Cretans' fight for freedom and independence. In the uprising of 1821, for example, the rebels inflicted a defeat on the Turks here. And earlier, in 1790, a single twenty-year-old, learning of the overbearing and aggressive behaviour of two Turkish janissaries in the town during some wedding festivities, had decapitated the pair of them before taking off for the mountains to begin life as a partisan. All in all, it was with some regret that I left this lively and attractive town the next morning at seven, under heavy clouds that were being sent scudding along by a high wind.

My planned route now took me off to the South-west for a while, in order to bring me down to the coast and to the Libyan Sea again, where I would renew my westward advance. The military ring to this statement is in fact a reflection of one trivial aspect of my behaviour at the time, for in order to help some of the longer, hotter miles to pass under my feet I occasionally took to explaining aloud to myself the strategy of the route ahead in my best imitation of Lord Montgomery – all sharp-throated and foxy upward cadences. I found that such mildly dotty exercises could provide a useful lift to the spirits when endurance over a lengthy period was called for.

There was 'Winterreise' to recite as well, of course, and other poetry. And there were times – for example during this particular day, much of it to be spent slogging along empty but shimmering tarmac in temperatures of at least the high nineties again, for a total of eleven and a half hours and thirty-five miles in all – when it was attractive to fall back on erotic fantasising. But then I would begin to wonder if the ensuing excitement was not in danger of detracting from, rather than adding to, my vigour, while in any case I find that an erection does tend to impede the free swing of the legs. Virtuously, therefore, I would seek to cool things off, both in my mind and, where possible, externally as well, with a good sousing of head and body from a village tap or farmer's hose. I am sure that Baden Powell, in whose memory and cause I had for some years, long before, weekly bared earnest knees amid the less-than-daring surroundings of the west Surrey commuter belt, would have been proud of me.

I took a narrow, minor road in order to cut off a corner by going through the hamlet of Frati, and as a consequence enjoyed an uplifting chat with a cheery and vigorous elderly lady who was climbing up to that village from the opposite direction. I enjoyed, too, the attentions of a shepherd's dog, who at first advanced with much display of menace and bared teeth, and then, when he saw that I was not greatly impressed, rolled over on his back to be tickled. Not the kind of behaviour to ensure the safety of his charges, but it made our shared world a nicer place, and the shepherd himself derived as much amusement from the performance as I did. Then, after a steep descent, I entered the deep and dramatic gorge of Kourtaliotiko, through which the wind was tearing with such force that my hat had to be returned to the safety of the rucksack.

Down below me as I emerged from the gorge was the road to Preveli monastery,[1] founded during the Middle Ages and one of the loveliest in Crete. Perched high above the Libyan Sea, this monastery, too, had always been centre of staunch resistance to the invader – Venetian, Turk, German. During the Second World War the monks selflessly aided British and Commonwealth troops who had been left behind following the defeat of 1941, while the Abbot himself, Father Agathangelos Langouvardos, a giant of a man, was obliged to leave the island altogether in order to escape German wrath. This stretch of coast, though, continued to be used as a rendezvous-point between Allied submarines or fast patrol boats on the one hand and escapees, agents, and partisans on the other.

The scenery in this part of Crete is very fine. 'One of the most retired and picturesque vales [in the island]', is how Spratt described the way down to the monastery; 'for crags of various forms, venerable and grey, beetle over gentle and swelling slopes; olive-grove glades, and open fields and vineyards in such proximity that a stranger's first impression on viewing it is to pronounce it the paradise of Crete. . . .'[2]

For me, however, the present day's business had to be of a rather sterner variety than I would expect to find in paradise. The Preveli monastery lay too far down and out of my way for me to visit it on this occasion. Instead, I swung back due west in

---

[1] That is, the 'piso Preveli' monastery, as distinct from the one, now abandoned, situated in a neighbouring valley.

[2] It will be apparent that this highly proficient and learned naval officer was not without a poetic touch. His compassion for the lepers he encountered in the island is notable (they were complete social outcasts at the time). And in another appealing paragraph he describes how, on one occasion when his ship was in Souda Bay, he thought he had caught sight of a mermaid ahead, only to discover on closer observation a seal tossing around a cuttlefish. 'The love of the romantic is apt to steal upon us all,' reflected the Captain subsequently, and asked: 'Why, then, should it be rejected (since it is so legitimately a part of the mind's exercise) when roving among these Classic lands and scenes?' *Travels and Researches in Crete, Vol. II*, pp. 133–5.

order to converge gradually with the coastline, in the process having to labour up a series of long, steep hills (the occasional downhill stretches made less impression on the mind) as the road snaked in and out of the mouths of yet more deep clefts in the mountain barrier to my right. The wind once again seemed always to oppose me, and once again my field of vision was reduced by my flattened hat-brim, as it had been on the very first day of the walk. A road-sign to Hora Sfakion frivolously, if not mockingly, deducted ten kilometres from the actual distance that lay ahead, though I was now no longer deceived by such idiosyncrasies. Once in a while a car would pass, but otherwise the only intrusion of human activity came when a group of three French cyclists suddenly sped by me from behind, their passing shouts of '*Salut!*', and mine in return, ringing incongruously around the mountain escarpments.

The clouds had all gone by now, and the heat grew intense (around 100°F again, I would say) as the wind at last died away. Slowly the road unwound before me: up from Mariou to Mirthios; through Sellia (where a costly fight with the Turks had taken place in 1869, and where a good many Turks, in their turn, were killed in 1896 as freedom drew near); through Rodakino – the way swooping down to the village only to zigzag steeply upwards immediately beyond. It was from the beach here, incidentally, that General Kreipe was finally taken off by submarine in 1944. In the upper part of Rodakino I was able to enjoy again the sight of an elderly woman sporting a single, long pigtail down her back, while on the edge of Argoules, a little further on, I spent some time over a drink in the enjoyable company of a couple of black-clad Sfakiot shepherds. (They were having great fun at the expense of the bar's attendant, aged about twenty-five, describing him for my benefit as a matheetees or young pupil – the joke was hung upon the contrast with my professorial status, which their questioning had elicited – on the grounds that he had been married for only a few months.)

On my right, the majestic bulk of the White Mountains began to rise to enormous heights: in all, containing fifty-seven peaks of 6–7,500 feet, with fifty-four lesser ones, the whole forming, in Fielding's words, 'a semi-circular stronghold . . . with the sea as a moat along its diameter.' Since Dorian times, at least, these mountains had provided shelter for rebels and the persecuted. (The island's Central Committee in 1895, making the natives' final, successful bid for freedom, had chosen a picture of these peaks for its seal.) The dramatic topography continues offshore, too, though unseen by the human eye, for hidden beneath the glittering waves is a chasm that more than matches the mountains themselves, being over 13,000 feet in depth.

I was now in the land of the Sfakiots, a people, as Spratt recorded it, who were 'a by-word among the lowland Cretans, for talents perverted, and for unscrupulous intrigue, theft, and cruelty . . . as well as for courage and patriotism.' Pashley, too, while being impressed by these last two qualities among the Sfakiots (Captain Manias, Pashley's guide in 1834 and pictured in the first of his two volumes, provides an excellent example of the breed), noted also the prevalence of blood-feuds, the readiness to kill on behalf of a friend, and the killing, also, of women deemed adulterous. It is in this region, concludes Spanakis, that the ancient customs of Cretan society are most fully preserved, not least its patriarchal nature. He suggests, too, that there even remain traces of those caste distinctions *within* the Sfakiot community itself which could restrict the choice of a marriage partner, for example. A tradition of hospitality, the notion of vengeance, a marked regional dialect with Dorian roots:[1] all remain in evidence to this day. And even when Sfakiots have been obliged to leave this part of Crete, or to depart the island altogether (as in 1821, when, under Turkish pressure, a good many moved to the much smaller island of Milos), they have taken their customs and traditions with them.

During that rising which began in 1821, the Sfakiot andartes inflicted much slaughter on the Turk in their inland regions, while on the coast they continued to exercise almost complete autonomy, some of the leading individuals concerned prospering

---

[1] I was interested to read Pashley's observation that it was among the women of Sfakia that this dialect was most marked, bearing in mind my own impression that the same broadly holds true for the sharper accents of New Zealand English: as in 'yis' for 'yes', for example.

greatly from their ship-borne trading. As for the near-legendary status of the Sfakiots in general, it is worth noting that although many observers – not least the island's own Kazantzakis[1] – have been struck by the regional differences of character among the people of Crete as a whole, there has not been unanimity among them regarding the respective characteristics involved. Thus, that sturdy Consul, William J. Stillman, concluded from his travels in the 1860s:

'The present inhabitants betray differences of character so great as almost to indicate differences of race. The Sphakiotes are larger of build, more restless and adventurous, thievish and inconstant, turbulent, and treacherous, than the people of any other region. The Selinotes, in the Westerly extreme [, however,] are the bravest of the Cretans, but less turbulent or quarrelsome, not given to stealing, and of good faith. In the eastern end, especially in the region of Gortyna and Gnossus [*sic*; "central-eastern" would have been a more accurate description], the blessings of the rule of Minos seem to rest in pacific natures.'

Be that as it may – and one can hear these matters being argued among Cretans today – I decided that I would not now extend my journey by a couple of miles in order to call in at one of Sfakia's well-known scenes of defiance: the fort of Frangokastello, originally built by the Venetians against raiding corsairs from North Africa. This was a much easier choice than the earlier one that had turned me aside from the summit of Psiloritis, for Frangokastello (the Frankish castle) has little that is attractive about it nowadays. Standing by the sea on the edge of a somewhat

---

[1] 'Kanea for weapons,' wrote Kazantzakis in *Freedom And Death*, 'Rethymnon for books, Megalokastro [Iraklion] for mugs.' Fielding, for his part, quotes the popular jingle: 'Men of Canea love to fight. Men of Rethymnon love to write. Men of Heraklion love their wine. Men of Lassithi [*sic*] – simply swine.' He adds the comment – unfair in my view – that 'The men of Lassithi are not so such swine as sheep. Everyone in Crete, excepting them, loves to fight; everyone, including them, loves his wine.'

bleak plain whose other boundary is the mountain-range itself, it is set about by summer campers, their cars, and purveyors of instant meals.

In its time, however, Frangokastello was the scene of much violent activity. Repeatedly attacked and sometimes destroyed by Cretan rebels, it was for a while abandoned altogether by the island's rulers as being too vulnerably situated to be worth restoring once more. Then in 1828 a band of rebels under Hadzimichalis Daliyannis (not himself a Cretan, but from the Morea) decided to stand and defy the Turk here, even though other, Cretan, captains had rightly opted to withdraw to where the mountains gave them the advantage over the large Turkish forces that were closing in. In one corner of the fort, in the chapel of Ayia Pelagia, 123 of Daliyannis' men were not only stationed but were chained together to ensure that there could be no question of retreat. All duly perished, while Hadzimichalis Daliyannis himself was beheaded by the Turks a week later, on 17th May, when they had brought their siege to a successful conclusion. Thereafter, only a few years had passed when Pashley found the event already commemorated in song, as if from the mouth of the hero himself:

> As once into the world I came,
> So, any one can tell,
> Then I, like every other man,
> Must bid it, once, farewell.
>
> And nobler 'tis that I should fall,
> Far nobler 'tis to die,
> Than that my honour should sustain
> Disgrace in every eye.

And so on. (The translation is Pashley's own.) Only a handful of the rebel garrison managed to escape by sea; but the wiser Sfakiots, who had declined to be isolated in the fort, thereafter inflicted great destruction on Mustapha Pasha's retiring Turks in their turn, the latter losing something like 1,700 men before their army had scrambled back to the safety of the island's northern shore. Daliyannis' decision to stand and fight in the fort had at least baited a fearsome trap, though matters had not been planned that way. And ever since, it is said – and many clearly believe it – when the atmospheric conditions in May are right, the sea is calm, and the sun has yet to rise, his blood-stained band appear on the foreshore, only to vanish seaward if approached or once the daylight has arrived.

Well, it was neither dawn nor May, and I ignored the turning down to the remains of the fortress. But I was prompted to reflect, as I continued my walk, on the question of how much substance and how much myth there has been over the centuries regarding the notion of a distinctive 'Europeanness'. The conjunction here of Greece and Venice (the latter, as I have indicated, so fierce in its repression of those it had colonised), together with my own Englishness, prompted the issue. So, too, did the Frenchness of a woman of about thirty-five (from Grenoble, it transpired) who, together with her son of about ten, came doggedly along the road from the opposite direction, hitchhiking around the South-west of the island. We found some shade and had an enjoyable chat in French (both of them were feeling the heat, even though they had come only the six miles from Hora Sfakion). Then I pressed on, wishing that I had alongside me my friend Peter Calvocoressi, scholar of both Greek and Italian descent, with whom to talk over these matters of the unifying and the divisive in European history and civilisation.[1]

I would have needed a rest, though, before trying to do justice to a conversation with Peter. And soon my mind was returning to more prosaic and immediate matters, and to the decision that thirty-five miles would be enough for the day. That meant that I could avoid having to stop in Hora Sfakion itself, with its coachloads of tourists, fresh (or not-so fresh) from their ramble down the Samarian gorge and their ensuing boat-trip from Ayia Rou-

---

[1] A further stimulus to such thoughts appeared almost immediately in the small village of Patsianos, where the sign above a tiny roadside building announced that here was a public library. To find a place of learning in so out-of-the-way a spot delighted me – though I am bound to add that the building in question was closed, and looked to have been so for some time.

meli. Instead I could put up for the night in a quiet, small village (population only about 150), just this side of it: in Komitades, which itself was of no little historical interest.

Komitades boasts a thirteenth-century Byzantine church, but the village as it now stands was built by members of the Venetian nobility. (Or so its inhabitants claim; Spanakis has reservations on the matter.) Situated at the foot of a steep ascent from the coast to the plain of Askifou above (from where a road runs across to the northern shore), the village and its neighbours were of some strategic importance over the years. Thus, for example, questions were asked in 1867, when Mustapha Pasha, the besieger of Arkadi, was able to take his army of suppression, which had landed from the sea at Frangokastello, up the slopes behind Komitades, unopposed, to join battle with rebel forces on the plain.

In May, 1941, though, it was about the British Army, and not least about its commanders, that questions were being asked in the neighbourhood of Komitades. For it was here that the remnants of the British, Australian, and New Zealand forces that had been defeated in the crucial battles around Hania came wearily down to the sea in the hope of evacuation, many of them exhausted by the trek across the mountains from the northern side of the island. Many, too, now faced the bitter disappointment of being told that insufficient shipping existed to take them off from Hora Sfakion (nearly 12,000 did get away to Egypt, but over 6,000 had to be left behind). It was a scene of no little confusion, as units – some still preserving discipline and spirit; others ragged and ready for bitterness – made their way down the sleep slope to Komitades. (The present, winding, metalled road did not then exist.) The more fortunate ones then passed on to Hora Sfakion a mile and a half or so along to the West.

'This island of disillusion' was how one of those present, Evelyn Waugh, was to sum up the experience in his *Officers and Gentlemen*, pointing above all towards signal failures of leadership; and one understands how that blandness, that ample layer of self-satisfied grease with which so many among the born-to-command strata of the English continue to coat themselves when seemingly in control, invited contempt when things fell apart with a vengeance. But it is clear, also – as Waugh's own novel acknowledges – that there were other officers who, whatever their social and educational background, continued to perform their duties with both courage and competence. In other words, as Antony Beevor concludes from his own careful study of the evidence, the behaviour among both officers and men varied greatly amid this unhappy and confused scene.

The formal surrender to the Germans of those troops left on shore took place in Komitades itself, though the village now appears to be devoid of any suggestion that it was once the scene of such dramas. I stopped at a kafeneion-cum-bar, and readily accepted its owner's offer of a room and supper – the latter consisting (there was no choice, and why should there have been) of salad and omelette, brought up the street by my host's wife from their house nearby. Whilst I was waiting, and over a tin of chilled grapefruit juice, I tried reading from a pile of local, Sfakiot newspapers that lay on one of the tables. But in my tired state I found myself bumping up against the limits of my Greek vocabulary even more frequently than usual. And so I was glad when the time came to make my way up a flight of outside stairs, on to the roof of the building, where my room, together with a separate toilet and washbasin, was situated.

It was a beautiful location. I looked out, over the thick vines that ran along the parapet, over the roof of the small church on the opposite side of the street, to the evening sea beyond. Although the voices of the few black-clad Sfakiots who sat on the street-side veranda below me continued to rise and fall (more often the former, of course), it was immensely peaceful. My left boot, like my left foot, was in urgent need of attention, while my once-white hat looked as if it had been washed in mud. But I had more breathtaking scenery lying ahead of me, together with my final major climb, over the White Mountains; and I could prepare for that particular challenge by essaying a lesser distance than usual, of about twenty-four miles or so, on the following day.

Once again, as I lay on my bed with foot-repairs completed,

the moonlight sent the white of the overhanging walls and the thick, Douanier-Rousseau black of the nearby power-cables spinning off into a variety of perspectives against the background of the night sky. The wind, which was warm off the sea – from the Libyan desert itself, I assumed – brought with it the sound of sheep's or goats' bells from somewhere down towards the fore-shore. When I went out on to the roof to visit the toilet for the last time before sleep, I could see the lights of some late coaches from Hora Sfakion, turning off nearby in order to climb slowly through the goose-necked bends of the road to the plain above – the reverse of that nightmare journey made by British and Commonwealth troops in 1941. Years before, I had done the same tourist stuff, and was grateful for the introduction to the island that it had given me. But I was glad, too, that I had moved on. And I felt sure, now, that barring a broken limb, and regardless of what might happen to boots or blisters, I would indeed complete the adventure that I had set for myself a year before.

CHAPTER SEVEN

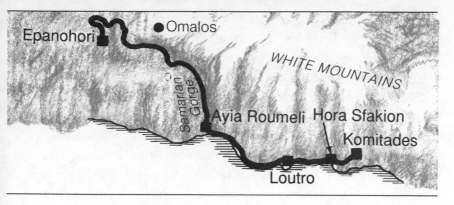

Komitades to Epanohori:
Samaria and beyond

I had decided that my crossing of the White Mountains, required by the self-imposed task of dealing with each of the five main blocks along my way, would take the form of climbing up the Samarian gorge, counter to the downward flow of tourists, to the plain of Omalos above. There were good reasons behind such a plan – not least the prospect of being silent and alone for some hours in the lower reaches of the gorge in all its beauty, free from alien voices.

If I were establishing the route again, however, I think I would try to follow, rather, one of the more remote tracks that wriggle their way over that forbidding bulk of limestone, even though this would involve looping much further to the North before turning westwards once more. Such a course would probably entail greater risks and challenges, as well as steering one entirely clear of the tourist tide. But at the time, my decision for the Samarian way was a firm one and seemed soundly based, and I therefore set out from Komitades in the last of the dark in order to head westwards, along the coastline towards Ayia Roumeli, where the famous gorge debouches on to the sea.

At first light I was passing through the small harbour-town of Hora Sfakion, scene of the British evacuation in 1941.

Destroyed by the Turks after an uprising in 1770, it had never quite recovered its former eminence in matters of trade, and now depends greatly on the tourist industry. A mile or so further on, where the metalled road to Anopolis begins its twisting climb away from the sea, I took, instead, a narrow, undulating footpath that led back down to the water's edge and to the beach at Sweetwater Bay – a stretch of pebbles obviously named from the fresh springs of mountain water that surface along and just off the shore. There was a scattering of small tents on the beach itself, together with a few sleeping-bags from which protruded tousled, somnolent heads. Only a solitary girl was about, eighteen or so and completely naked, wandering off to collect some of the natural water-supply in a plastic bottle. She seemed to be shut away in a world of her own, almost in a daze, and we passed by each other with scarcely a nod, my pack-weighted boots sinking loudly and purposefully into the shingle in contrast to the slow, elfin meanderings of her bare feet. I felt a trifle oafish, but there it was.

At the end of Sweetwater, the path climbs once more, though never straying far from the sea in negotiating a series of rocky undulations and before descending into the tiny resort of Loutro a mile or so further on. Loutro offers its own version of lotus-land, its few houses and tavernas rimming a semi-circular cove, its supplies brought in by the ferry from Hora Sfakion. Xan Fielding, visiting it for the first time after the war, found it a more easy-going, a less swaggeringly macho community than any he had known in Crete. Over the centuries, however, it has not escaped the turmoil of the island's struggles for independence. Closely linked with the village of Anopolis on the mountain-side above (itself the home of Daskaloyiannis, a wealthy trader who was the hero of the vain uprising of 1770), Loutro and its tiny harbour served for a time as the seat of the Revolutionary Commission of 1821 and as a storage place for artillery pieces. Hussein Pasha therefore descended on the place with a large force, only to find that the rebels had set fire to their guns and equipment rather than see them fall into Turkish hands. And although many of the inhabitants of both Loutro and Anopolis then felt obliged to leave Crete altogether, the rebels of 1866 again brought cannon here by sea in order to defy the oppressor once more.

It was about nine o'clock when I reached Loutro, and I decided to indulge in a fuller breakfast than usual, at one of the small restaurants that line the beach. Already it promised to be another extremely hot day, and I filled myself with as much orange-juice as I could decently consume, as well as replenishing two of my three water-bottles. Then I climbed out of the cove, over the hill behind, on which there stand both the remains of a Turkish fort and traces of the Roman city of Phoenix. Legend has it that it was here at Phoenix that St Paul, having landed during his enforced journey to Rome itself, began to seek potential converts, and thereupon was beaten up by locals for being a busybody.

The entire Pauline legend in these parts was carefully explored by Spratt, who brought to bear on it his expertise in matters of seamanship and navigation. The apostle's ship did indeed call in at Crete (see *Acts*, 27)[1], but further to the East at Fair Havens, now Kali Limenes. And although it seems that its captain did then seek to reach the greater shelter of Loutro/Phoenix – and Spratt's reasoning remains persuasive – it is likely that strong winds forced the vessel on and out, past its immediate goal and past the remainder of Crete altogether, towards Malta and eventual shipwreck.

My own course westwards began to require a degree of effort at this stage, some of it gratuitous in that I wrongly suspected that the path on from Phoenix must lie high above the water-line. I climbed steeply, therefore, only to discover half a mile or so further on that a deep ravine, lying across my line of advance, obliged me to descend to the beach once more, where I duly picked up the track I had been searching for. As visitors who take

---

[1] See also St Paul's letter to Titus, first bishop of the Church in Crete. It is here that Paul cites the Cretan philosopher, Epimenides, as saying that 'The Cretans are always liars, evil beasts, slow bellies', adding the comment: 'This witness is true. Wherefore rebuke them sharply.' The philosophic complexities that reside in a Cretan's avowal that all Cretans are liars do not appear to have troubled the writer or mitigated his own swingeing condemnation. St Paul has always seemed to me to rank fairly high among the reasons for not belonging to a Christian church.

the Ayia Roumeli–Hora Sfakion ferry will know, the coastline here presents a somewhat harsh aspect. Pashley, descending into Loutro by horse, found the loose and jagged rocks constituted a trap which threw over and badly gashed his animal, while Spratt, faced with the series of alternating ravines and ridges, concluded that this was 'a magnificent but somewhat forbidding part of Crete.' Even Pendlebury conceded, 'The going [here] is hard.' It was not surprising, then, when I encountered a party of young Americans, their leader in good enough form but the remainder exhausted and straggling. They were travelling from Ayia Roumeli to Loutro, and had taken, up to that point where we met, getting on for two hours longer than I was about to require in the reverse direction. The lesson will bear repetition: it is not advisable to wander into the Cretan landscape, in the summer months especially, unless fully prepared physically, mentally, and in terms of equipment.

The temperature was by now back up in the region of 100°F or so, and the harsh, shadeless nature of the terrain exacerbated matters. A sense of desiccation prevailed, even there beside the Libyan Sea: a sense equalled in my own experience only once in Uttar Pradesh after a long period of drought, once when four-wheel-driving in the central Australian desert to the East of Alice Springs, and rather more frequently in the committee proceedings of a certain academic assembly back in Britain. It was easy to believe that people could begin to hallucinate if exposed too long to such conditions – perhaps a partial explanation, I surmised, of why the Sfakiots of the region have possessed a long-standing belief in vampires, as recorded in some detail by Pashley among others.

Clearly, I needed to take additional precautions (against dehydration, that is; the vampires would have to be responded to ad hoc) before moving on, and doubly so in that my needless climbing after Phoenix had induced me to consume already about a third of my water supply. I therefore looked around as I followed the rocky, steeply undulating path until I spotted what looked like a shepherd's well, some 200 metres below me in the direction of the mockingly cool waves. Scrambling steeply down, the seat of my once-again-filthy shorts, as well as my battered boots, having to take the strain, I found that this time I had got it right: a covered well with the usual empty olive-tin on its long rope nearby. The well looked as if it had not been used for some time, but it served to provide a series of showers – the gallon-or-so tinful poured repeatedly over my head – and a refill (with water-purifying tables added as a precaution) for all three of the bottles I was carrying with me.

Then it was on again until the track sloped back down, through the beginnings of a pine wood, to the water's edge, and to the beautiful little church of St Paul – 'like a valuable casket', in the words of one Professor Dawkins, 'accidentally dropped on the shore.' This, is it suggested, was the site where the apostle baptised his Cretan converts, making use of a small spring beside the sea; and this, too, is supposedly the spot where he also found time to banish from the entire island all noxious creatures such as snakes (a purpose which, alas, he did not quite fulfil in its entirety).

Whatever the truth of this (and of course, if Spratt's argument is accepted, it is no more – and no less – than myth), the next half mile or so proved to be some of the hardest going of the entire journey. For my way led past the red-tiled church, and along a beach of fine grey sand into which my weight of around 230 lbs in all, pack and self combined, sank deeply down. (I was to find that I had shed seven pounds during the walk as a whole.) Even then I could find little purchase from which to drive the legs for the next step forward. The sand began to lip over the high ankles of my boots. The sweat began to pour down into my eyes, simply swamping the band that stretched across my forehead. With a brief pause for an apology to St Paul (one never knows, after all), I resorted to a prolonged and emphatic use of the language of the lower deck – echoes from my time in the aircraft-carrier *Indefatigable* over thirty-five years earlier – in order to help drive myself on, until at last the path lifted up, off the end of the beach, and climbed back among the pine trees once more.

My arrival in Ayia Roumeli, therefore, even though the journey of twenty-three or twenty-four miles from Komitades had lasted only eight hours, was a welcome one. Already, the hamlet, with its small collection of restaurants and tavernas, was beginning to fill with the walkers who had come down the Samarian gorge that morning. But I tucked myself away in the cool of an upstairs room and surveyed the damage. The outside of my left heel was still defying all my attempts to get it to mend and to cease blistering anew, but the main danger appeared to lie elsewhere:

> 'Have just tried to fix what is now problem/threat number one,' I wrote in my journal an hour or two later. 'The sole/bottom layer of both boots is threatening to come off. . . . Left foot is still bad, but I can MAKE that last. Not surprising: they [feet and boots] have taken a fearful bashing, and today was as bad as any for them.'

The 'fixing' in question required that I should first brave the milling throng of gorge-walkers (far more of them then when I had first made the descent seven or eight years before) in order to obtain from a neighbouring 'mini-market' a tube of superglue, thus obviating the need to try to secure the soles of my boots with the strong tapes that formed part of my emergency kit. (Superglue itself has since joined the list of essential items, of course.) A shower and change of clothes then had their usual restorative effect, as did several cartons of chilled orange-juice, after which there was time to rest in preparation for my climb up the gorge itself the following morning. After the long spells of solitude that I had enjoyed since leaving Kato Zakros (had it been no more than eleven days before?), I felt uncomfortable even with the sounds of the crowds of tourists below my window. But the six o'clock ferry to Hora Sfakion brought a sudden peace.

'*Was vermeid ich denn die Wege, wo die andern Wandrer gehn . . . ?*' Lying in bed later on, after eating in the taverna downstairs, I spoke silently to myself about the need to avoid becoming unduly unsociable and a Schubertian shunner of crowds. The noise of a two-stroke engine, powering a small and dilapidated three-wheeled truck that was used to haul crates of bottles and other stores to and from the ferries, conjured up further memories of India, but then spluttered back into silence. The local midges, being Sfakiot, were intent on demonstrating that no insect-repellent in the world could deter their attacks. But not even their insistent attentions, nor a sudden and brief volley of gunfire that echoed around the hamlet, could prevent my drifting off into a tired but exuberant sleep.

The ancient village of Ayia Roumeli lies in fact not alongside the tavernas and gift-shops beside the beach, but a mile or so up the Samarian gorge. The historic town of Tara (or 'Tarrha', in Pashley's rendering) was sited somewhere close by, while despite the tendency for malaria to stalk the locality the Sfakiots based trading ships here in later years. During the nineteenth century, too, the area around and behind the beach witnessed much revolutionary activity. Refugees from all parts of Sfakia assembled here in 1866, only to be bombarded by three Turkish warships – though the enemy troops who then landed in force failed to capture the women and children, who had retreated up the gorge, and suffered considerable casualties themselves. Again in the following year the Turks landed here, this time with 4,000 men; but again, although they burned Ayia Roumeli itself, they failed to pass through the narrow 'gates' where the sheer 1,500 feet cliffs on either side of the gorge squeeze to within about ten feet of each other, and thus did not penetrate the main body of the chasm beyond. In August of that same year, 1867, the ship *Arkadi*, already mentioned as being funded by British sympathisers for the Cretan cause, arrived to bring artillery and food supplies, while taking off more refugees at the same time. Two Turkish warships then appeared, however, and although the *Arkadi* was able to convey the women and children westwards and land them near Paleohora, she was then trapped by the enemy. Her captain set fire to the ship, but the Turks succeeded in putting out the flames and towed the *Arkadi* off to Istanbul as a prize.

Notable occurrences to the seaward side of Ayia Roumeli did not end here. For example it was from this beach that King George of Greece, together with ministers, British officers and diplomats, and his British mistress, left Crete on 22nd May 1941, on board the Royal Navy destroyer *Decoy*. (They had travelled across the island ahead of the advancing Germans and then journeyed round from Hora Sfakion by small boat.) But it is, above all, with the wooded depths of the Samarian gorge itself (where timber was still cut until 1965) that the Cretan characteristics of defiance and self-sufficiency are particularly associated. For the gorge – at about twelve miles long the largest in Europe, and impassable in winter owing to the torrent that rushes along its length from the White Mountains to the sea – has been a home for rebel bands[1], as well as for robbers and convicts on the run, and a frequent refuge for the women and children of Sfakia. 'The villagers,' recorded Pashley, 'point with exaltation to the lofty mountains by which they are surrounded, and say that they are the best fortress to be found in all Crete.' And, indeed, as mentioned earlier, the gorge was again to prove a secure refuge in 1867, although in 1868, following an act of betrayal on someone's part, the Turks did at last gain access to it, and forced many starving rebels to surrender.

Many thousands of visitors from all over Europe and even further afield have now been able to enjoy the splendours of the gorge[2], thanks to its new status as a National Forest, and to the care with which its pathway is now kept in good repair. 'I doubt if, in the range of habitual travel, there is another such scene,' wrote Consul Stillman when he returned for one last visit to Crete in July 1869 before leaving for the United States. Peering down from the top of the gorge, he observed: 'It was as if the mountains had gaped to their very bases', while on descending

---

[1] The island's Communists made their final stand here, too, during the civil war that followed World War Two.

[2] I exclude from this description those (they are in many cases Greek, I fear) who descend to the loud accompaniment of transistor radios. If I term them philistines, I must add that they should not be confused with the historic people of that name, who settled in the Near East, possibly having passed through Crete itself.

part of the way into the chasm itself he revelled in 'the balsamic odors of firs and pine.' Pashley, too, 35 years earlier, had been mightily impressed by 'the glories' of the scene, departing with sadness after travelling only a short way up from the seaward end. 'I am indeed leaving,' he quoted,

> A land whose azure mountain tops are seal
> For Gods in council; whose green vales, retreats
> Fit for the shades of heroes, mingling there
> To breathe Elysian peace in upper air.

My own journey up through this magnificent scenery began at seven in the morning, and for the next two hours or so I was entirely alone. The only sounds were the wind in the pines, the occasional splashing of the stream, and the echoing blows of my bastouni on the rocks. No rays of sun penetrated the gorge at that hour, of course, but there were spectacular glimpses to be had of them striking the peaks far above. Cool and clean after the squalor of the previous day, my boots freshly glued back into order and my pack reduced to about 30 lbs in the knowledge that sources of fresh water lay ahead, I began to let my self-imposed injunction of σιγα σιγα (slowly, slowly) be overtaken by the exhilaration of it all, and by the high degree of mechanical efficiency which my preparation, and now the walk itself, had brought to my grandfatherly frame. Pausing only occasionally, where the path crossed and recrossed the stream, to wet my head and neck in the icy water, I found my legs propelling me upwards with a shepherd-like spring, the bastouni striking more rapidly and aggressively into the steadying rocks along the way.

Eventually, of course, the procession of tourists who had set out from the top around dawn began to appear. But, as I wrote in my journal a few hours later,

> 'it wasn't as awful as I'd feared. Many youngish couples (the French looking very organised, and usually in larger groups); the Brits amateurish and

amiable; the Greeks talking like mad, and tending to lag behind. Smells of toothpaste, of sun cream – and, from one middle-aged couple who looked as if they hadn't exercised for a while, I'd swear of mothballs – all fleetingly overcoming those of the pines and the morning crispness. Much standing aside and "ooh la'ing" from the French; "you must be joking" from a jocular, unfit, middle-aged Brit; and so on.'

Looking back now, I suspect that by this time my vigorous momentum, born of fitness and sheer delight, also owed something to an enjoyment at being the odd person out, proceeding up the mountain rather than down it with the multitude. At all events, it suddenly dawned on me, as I passed by the church of Ayios Nikolaos (constructed on the site of a temple to Apollo, and flanked by fine cyprus trees) that I was going to reach the summit only four hours or so after leaving my beach-side lodgings. The final stage of the climb that now lay ahead was by far the steepest, zigzagging upwards by a series of carefully constructed steps. (The total drop from the top to the floor of the gorge, via this 'wooden ladder', is one of about 3,000 feet.) But the notion of getting inside the four-hour mark began to take a hold of me, while there was something pleasantly familiar about the rivulets of sweat that began to pour off me as I set to with a new abandon.

I was rescued from my surrender to this somewhat silly preoccupation with hours and minutes by an encounter with one of the gorge's park-rangers, who was sitting by one of the wayside water-sources that have been prepared for visitors. 'Up, not down!' he said with a smile, and when, in response to his question, I told him what time I had left the beach area – πολυ ωραια!' – 'That's splendid!' Had I come round to Ayia Roumeli by boat? he then asked. And so, of course, I had to explain about the walk as a whole. A nice man; an enjoyable interlude after the intensity of the climb – and four hours ten minutes to the gate at the top in consequence: an untidy total which, I reflected, had put matters back into their proper perspective after all.

I paused at the summit to consume large quantities of chilled drinks at the kiosk nearby, walked a mile or so down the metalled road to where the high plain of Omalos opened out before me, turned off westwards once more along a dirt-track, and was soon stretched out on a patch of dense, short grass that might almost have come from the South Downs themselves. I had climbed the last of my five mountain blocks. The steep ridges and the final mountain rim of Western Crete still awaited me, ensuring that the hard work was far from over. But it was another good moment, nonetheless.

The plain of Omalos, or 'the Omalo', stands around 3,500 feet above sea level and, like Katharo and Nidha to the East, can be used only during the summer months. Between a mile and a half and two miles across, it is fertile. And like the gorge below it has long served as a place of refuge and a centre of defiance for Cretans wishing to remain free – during the struggles of the 1820s, for example. During the uprising of the 1860s it produced a notable nationalist leader in the person of Hadzimichalis Iannaris – not to be confused with the Hadzimichalis Daliyannis who had died heroically at Frangokastello forty years earlier. In the Second World War, too, the people of the plain provided succour to those resisting the German occupation, the Germans in return executing 110 men here (a good many of them not active partisans; six of them British military personnel) in September 1941.[1]

It was to a spot close by the Omalo, also, that I had come

---

[1] Again, however, the internecine ferocity of Cretans must be recalled also. As I climbed out of the plain to the West, I passed the little church of Saint Theodore. And here, beside it, are the graves of two Pendaris brothers: friends of Xan Fielding during the early stages of the war, but killed thereafter as part of a clan feud with the Sartjetis family from Selino. This one feud, which began in 1943 (over a theft, perhaps, or a rape?), had by 1952 cost over 80 men their lives according to Fielding, who revisited the area in that year.

some years before on the directions of George Psychoundakis, in order to see where one of the most remarkable individuals to take part in the island's struggles against the Germans had been ambushed and killed in 1944: the New Zealander, Dudley Perkins, or 'Vasili' as he was known locally.

Only the evening before, over supper in Ayia Roumeli, I had been telling two New Zealand girls about him. (They had walked down the gorge, and then decided to stay the night where they were.) They had never heard of him before, but seemed interested and impressed – like the university audiences in their country when I have brought Perkins into my lectures there on the Second World War. ('Europe' spreading outwards from Crete, eventually to reach its most distant outpost in New Zealand – at the expense of the Maoris, of course; then Perkins coming back from the mountains of South Island to the mountains of Crete, to fight and to die: it is an obvious, but, to my mind, striking way of looking at it.)

Born in Otago the son of an Anglican parson, Perkins broke off his university studies in 1939 in order to volunteer for the Army. Having taken part in the retreat from the mainland of Greece, he was one of those in Crete who failed to obtain a place on the ships evacuating Hora Sfakion, after which he quickly escaped from the flimsy prison camp into which he and his colleagues had been herded by the victorious Germans. For over a year thereafter he was on the run in the mountains of western Crete, before he was eventually taken off by submarine to Egypt. There, having walked out of officer-training school (apparently scornful of its petty ways), he arranged to train with Special Operations Executive and returned to Crete under their aegis, as a Staff Sergeant, in July 1943.

Back in the island, Perkins operated principally in the Selino region that I was myself about to enter, and notably with a band of andartes centred on the village of Koustoyerako.[1] Among

---

[1] It was from the hillside above this village that Kostas Paterakis fired his celebrated shot to kill the officer of a German detachment that was about to murder by machine-gun fire a line of women and children in the square below. The Germans destroyed the village during the later stages of the occupation.

these men he established a reputation as a staunch and fearless comrade: a true pallikari who, for example, led a notably successful attack on a German patrol that had been surrounded in a cheese-making hut near the village. To the Germans themselves, he became worth a price on his head. To Xan Fielding, his commander in the region, he was simply 'the bravest man I have ever had the honour to meet.[1]'

Fielding's successor, however, a British officer of Greek but not Cretan descent, thought less of Perkins' achievements, while seeming not to have got on with the Cretans themselves either. His order that Perkins should leave the island was refused by the New Zealander, who did agree, however, in February 1944, to travel across the mountains, close by the Omalo, in order to discuss the matters at issue. Possibly there then took place an act of betrayal within the setting of the tangled politics of what were sometimes rival Cretan bands. At all events, a ring of about fifty German troops was lying in wait for Perkins and his few companions as they toiled up the hillside of Stepanoporo.

Only recently turned twenty-nine years of age, but a natural and entirely unassuming leader, the New Zealander stood, firing defiantly, until killed. To the anger of the Germans, the villagers nearby covered and re-covered his makeshift grave with flowers. He lies buried now in the British and Commonwealth war cemetery at the head of Souda Bay. He would have rejoiced, I am sure, to know that several hundred people of Cretan descent now live on the other side of the world, in New Zealand itself, as a result of alliances contracted between fellow soldiers and young women of the island during the war.

My own route now took me back in the opposite direction to the one followed by Perkins in his ill-fated approach to the Omalo: along a dirt road towards the Selino valley that had been a paved thoroughfare in Roman times. The way looped northwards for a while, as it dropped down from the western edge of the White Mountains, then swung sharply south on

---

[1] Perkins was recommended for the award of a Victoria Cross, but denied it because his feats had not been witnessed by an officer: another triumph for the strong element of snobbism within the British social system.

joining the metalled road from the North, close to where a ridge offers commanding views of both coasts of the island. (Pashley, in 1834, marvelled at what could be seen from the spot.) By five in the afternoon I had reached the scattered village of Epanohori, on my way back down to the Libyan Sea: only twenty-three miles or so covered, but of course they had included Samaria, and I felt I had done enough for that day. In any case, another session with the superglue was urgently called for. I was happy, therefore, to find once more a taverna that offered a room up on its roof – and once more a beautiful view to go with it: this time southwards, out over the usual fringe of vines, towards the sea near Souyia.

For the final time, the French thread reappeared in my journey, on this occasion in the shape of a family of four who were doing some walking locally on this, their first visit to the island. And again, as in the boarding house in Kamares, there was the switching of languages to cope with and enjoy, as I explained over our common supper table to both these fellow-northerners and the local 'lads' what I had been up to, and how the once deeply ridged soles of my boots had become worn nearly smooth. It felt a European evening with which to end a day to remember.

CHAPTER EIGHT

Epanohori to the
Monastery of Hrisoskalitissas:
not the end of the road

The western extremities of Crete, like their eastern counterparts, are seldom explored by visitors, and indeed remain unfamiliar to a good many of the island's own inhabitants. Topographically speaking, this south-western corner that I was now walking through did make an impression on Captain Spratt, however, as he observed with an expert eye its brown, red, and purple shales, and the masses of grey limestone gouged by the movement of water into a series of alternating narrow ridges and steep-sided valleys. ('The wildest and most picturesque part of the coast of Crete' was how he judged the shore itself east of Selino.)

'Nothing can be more uncomfortable, in [sic] a military point of view, than one of these Cretan ravines,' noted Consul Stillman after travelling in these parts. 'Cut into the limestone rock by the glacier torrents of ages, zigzag in their courses, and shut between abrupt ridges. . . .' It was steady but not easy going, therefore, as I followed the deserted, switchback road (first met-alled, then dirt) south-westwards, through Irtakina and Azoyires, towards the coastal town and beach resort of Paleohora.

This is a region, moreover, that, however little it is explored today, is rich in historical associations. Irtakina itself, for example, like Kandanos that lay just north of my route and like

127

Lissos, Souyia, and Selino/Paleohora on the coast, had been a notable city in its time. As for the resolute contribution down the centuries of the Selinots as a whole to the cause of Cretan independence, this has already been noted through the comments of Consul Stillman. In Dudley Perkins' village of Koustoyerako, for instance, there was numbered among his band – and there remains to this day – a descendant of George Kandanoleon, who was put to death for leading a rebellion against the Venetians in 1527.

The uprising against the Turks in the 1820s also had strong roots in this part of Crete, and indeed a good many of the roadside trees along my way carried posters advertising an exhibition to commemorate one of the captains, or leaders, from that time, Manolis Theodorakis. Likewise, in May 1941, an ad hoc force was led out from Paleohora and along the road towards the fighting in the North by the village priest, Papa Stylianos Frantzekakis, a man clearly from the same mould as his confrères in Anoyia, Arkadi, Preveli and Vrondissi. Meeting German motor-cycle units coming in the opposite direction near Kandanos, Papa Frantzekakis' band succeeded in holding up the enemy for some time. (Kandanos itself was duly levelled to the ground by the barbarian invaders, to the accompaniment of the usual executions.)

I must admit, though, that there were times during this day's walking – and again the temperature was up in the high nineties at least – when my mind turned to matters more immediate and mundane than the cities of the past or the heroism of the people: in brief, to dogs.

Now I like to think that I get on well with dogs in general, and indeed have had a number of splendid relationships in this regard: not with the short-legged, yappy kind favoured in certain elevated circles, that is, but with proper dogs of the large and hairy variety. In Crete itself, I have usually established excellent relations with the dogs of my shepherd friends, once they have gone through their initial and required routine of aggressive posturing. (It is true, though, that I have one friend, Manolis Parasiris – yet another member of that extensive family – whose dog, even though he now reluctantly accepts that I am to be classed as non-threatening, still eyes my passing legs from time to time as if they were a brisola – a cutlet – of some kind.) Of course, as Rendel and other clandestine operatives have noted, to walk through a village, especially outside the hours of daylight, is to invite a mongrels' chorus to sound forth; but the animals themselves seldom threaten any harm. So it does not surprise me that Edward Lear, whose experiences with shepherds' dogs while sketching in Albania were at times alarming in the extreme, found the dogs of Crete amiable by comparison.

I have to say, however, that the animals who greeted my passage along some of these Selinot stretches of the journey were of an altogether different disposition, outdoing even those restless creatures who figure in the Müller/Schubert passages I quoted earlier. Several were Alsatians, or nearly related to that breed. But I suspect that their ferocity owed not a little to their immediate circumstances, for often they were being kept chained up with a heat-absorbing, up-ended oil drum for a kennel. Whatever the cause, they would come flying out at me, only to be brought up short by their chain (if chained they were), or by my levelled bastouni if they were free to range further afield. Things never actually came to blows, but the proceedings did serve to put an edge on my senses, as the heat and a succession of steep hills threatened to dull my spirits a little.

A few miles above Paleohora, the dirt-track that I was following wound its way through dense glades not only of olives (great bundles of black nets lying around their trunks, ready for use in the harvesting), but also of trees of many different kinds. I rested for a while in this delightful setting. Then I passed on down into Paleohora itself, its eastern end almost deserted on this hot and sleepy Saturday afternoon, with the crowds enjoying the beach on the other side of town. I stopped again, to eat, drink and doze for a while on a bench by the sea wall, looking back eastwards to where the White Mountains plunged directly and dramatically into the sea. Ayia Roumeli itself was out of sight, around a distant headland; but I had completed my large loop to the North, over the range and then back down again to the coastline. Now I would stay by the sea – or rather seas – to my journey's end.

A Venetian castle was built here in Paleohora in the late thirteenth century by the Duke of Crete himself, who called it 'Selino', which in turn became the name of the province. Thereafter, the castle was seized by Cretan rebels, recaptured and rebuilt by the Venetians in 1334, taken and destroyed by pirates in the early sixteenth century, seized by the Turks in their turn in the seventeenth century, then destroyed by them once more as being too vulnerable and tempting to leave standing. An everyday story of Cretan life down the centuries, one might say. In a way more remarkable still is the fact that the area where the town now stands was once, into Roman times, under water; for it will be recalled that a shift in the earth's plates had then heaved up this end of the island by as much as twenty-six feet in places. It must have been a terrifying experience for those living here at the time.

By now it was extremely hot, but despite this, and despite the temptations of the town (it even boasts a cinema), I decided to push on to Koundoura, a village, or rather a scattering of houses, about four or five miles to the West. I wanted to reduce the distance that I would have to cover on the following, final day of the journey, for I intended to leave enough time over to travel back down the island by a succession of buses to my base in Elounda. In the event I had more than the direct distance to Koundoura to cover, in that it took some traipsing up and down the road there, retracing my steps by a mile or more, before I could find a room for the night. And I subsequently walked another couple of miles to the only available telephone and back, in order to report to the Adamakis family back in the East that I hoped to see them again before the morrow was out.

While going through this last process, I found that I still possessed sufficient patience to cope with the remarkable vagaries of the Cretan telephone system, and thus knew that I also retained ample resources for the final climb over the island's western mountain rim. Indeed, the twenty-six or so miles that I had covered that day (including my meanderings at the end) now seemed rather little. I also, in my insouciance, shrugged off the fact that I had allowed my stock of wound-dressings to run dangerously low (the pharmacies in Paleohora had been closed for the afternoon when I was passing through). But I was to be brought down to earth when, having used the last of them to dress once again the mess on my left heel, I cut a finger quite deeply while opening a tin of corned beef that I had purchased for my supper. So, bloodied handkerchief had to join inner-socks and underpants in the bathetic ensemble worn for my final evening's rest on top of my bed.

Two local details lent to this last stop a certain symmetry with the walk's beginning – a beginning that, as I noted in my journal, now seemed two months rather than two weeks away. One was that a further array of electronic intelligence aerials loomed over me on the hills above Koundoura, just as they had near Ziros – both being a reminder (together with the heavily laden shipping that I could see passing eastwards off this corner of the island) of the Gulf crisis that had been mounting during my time out of circulation. The other was provided by the copy of the *Guardian* that I had bought while passing through Paleohora – the only issue that I had read since that first night in Xerokambos. Browsing through the paper had the same effect as my telephone call to Elounda: I felt far removed from such worlds, and wanted still to think only in terms of distances, gradients, water-supplies, and the translating of my immediate needs into Greek. I began to suspect that a period of readjustment might lie ahead.[1]

The final day, or rather part-day, of my journey was to prove a delight in terms of the walking that was involved. My hopes of a reunion with Theodoti Kolokotronis were also to be fulfilled. And a totally unforeseen and beneficent twist was given to one of the themes that had been building up in my head over the previous two weeks. What more could I have asked?

[1] I was indeed to feel disorientated for a while after my return to Elounda. And the endorphins, or whatever they were, in my system continued for some weeks, both in Crete and back in England, to rouse me before dawn, whispering insistently that exercise would be an excellent idea. So the gentle turf of the South Downs had to help cushion my withdrawal symptoms.

When I had inquired during the previous evening about the route around the south-west corner of the island and then up to the monastery of the Golden Stairway, Moni Hrisoskalitissas, I had been pointed in a rather vague way towards the horizon a couple of miles away, where the final shoulder of mountain-side softened into mere hills before running down into the sea. That had seemed good enough to be going on with, especially since my map clearly showed an unmetalled road winding all the way from Koundoura to the monastery. Loading up for the last time, I was off at six-fifteen, just as it was beginning to get light. I paused only to make my farewells to the parents of the lodging-house's owner, who were already up and dressed, sitting in silent companionship on their balcony and looking (wistfully? content-edly? nostalgically? unfeelingly? I wondered) towards the distant mountains and the dawn.

The metalled road soon came to an end, and the ensuing dirt-road to the West began to zigzag its way among a succession of large, plastic-covered hot-houses for the growing of tomatoes and suchlike. Thereafter, however, the dirt-road itself announced in its turn that it was about to peter out, and I was left to puzzle over the exact line to take over the hill that lay ahead. The map, in other words, had once again proved not simply inadequate, but actively deceitful. I therefore looked to where some kind of gully seemed to run up towards the brow of the hill, inland and slightly to my right, and made in that direction.

Before long I could see that I had chosen wrongly, however, for I found myself having to clamber over a succession of wire-mesh fences which, if I failed to clear them entirely, were under threat of being flattened by the somewhat tank-like advance of myself, my pack, and my bastouni. Fortunately, though, help was at hand in the shape of a couple of early-morning hunters (it was a Sunday), who had already begun to bang away on the lower ground that lay between myself and the sea. There was no road to the monastery, they confirmed; but there was a narrow path which was marked (again) by a succession of red dots on the rocks, and which began down at the end of the beach below us. I was properly under way at last.

The path and its dots were there all right; and although during the two-to-three hours that followed there were to be times when both the markings and the worn-down line of the track itself were easily lost to view amid the rocks and scrub, it was only a matter of climbing up to the nearest prominence to be able to look back down and pick up the way ahead once more. It proved to be another switchback ride, but a far more entertaining one than that between Epanohori and Paleohora on the previous day. Then it had simply been a matter of following a road along its succession of ascents and descents. This time, the path would snake its way in and out of rocky protuberances, dive down to a shingle beach and then, with only a splash of paint or a small cairn of stones to beckon one on, soar suddenly up to cross over and behind a high ridge, where a finger of the western mountain-barrier had all at once advanced itself to the very coastline.

The sounds of the hunters' guns died away; the sun, away to my right now that I had turned the corner of the island and was heading only a little west of north, lifted itself high enough to spread a glittering path across the Mediterranean down on my other hand. I was utterly alone, with not a dwelling or sign of life to be seen in any direction. And I was quietly and extremely happy.

The only sombre thoughts that flitted across my mind concerned that new stretch of sea to my left. For it was out there, to the west of Crete, that the Royal Navy had suffered great losses in May 1941 as a consequence of total German air-superiority during the battle for, and evacuation of, the island. It was there, for example, that the egregious Mountbatten's destroyer *Kelly* had gone down under Stuka attack – as subsequently dramatised in Noël Coward's film, *In Which We Serve*. And it was in the context of such rapidly mounting losses that the Commander-in-Chief of the Mediterranean Fleet, Admiral Sir Andrew Cunningham, was urged to withdraw units which had become almost totally vulnerable; in this context, too, that he declined, with the observation that while it took the Navy three years to build a new ship, it had taken it 300 to build its reputation.

Meanwhile, the final section of the splendid path required one last climb over the shoulder of an amiably modest mountain. Then it took me down, in an increasingly ill-defined series of swerves between bushes, trees and scrub, to the suddenly broader coastal plain, on the edge of which stood the monastery I was seeking. Passing what looked like a long-unused field-chapel at the foot of the mountain, I joined soon afterward the dusty, potholed road (now, at last, the map regained a degree of veri-similitude) that runs from the monastery and its adjoining scat-tering of houses to the beach at Elafonisis. Here I came across my first people since the hunters of Koundoura: a cheerful family who had come out in their pick-up truck to harvest their carob trees. And from them I received, not only cold water (poured over my head and shoulders, as I requested, from the tailgate of the truck), but the warming news that Theodoti Kolokotronis was alive and well, and still residing in the monastery.

The monastery of the Golden Stairway, perched on rocks immediately above an inlet of the sea, derives its name from the belief that the ninety stone steps leading up to its cloisters were once made of gold, or, alternatively, that one of them remains golden – though this fact cannot be perceived by those without faith. As yet another religious centre for nationalist resistance, the monastery was a place of refuge under the Venetians. And legend has it that during the 1820s uprising against the Turks, enemy soldiers who had carried out a massacre in a neighbouring village were driven off from the sacred building itself by a swarm of vengeful Cretan bees. Certainly, Allied soldiers were given succour here after their defeat at German hands in the summer of 1941. The Germans themselves, having driven out the resident monks, then established a prison in the buildings in 1943, partly for their own military offenders.

The tradition of self-supporting nuns residing in The Golden Stairway is also a lengthy one. Fifteen or so such women were here in the nineteenth century, living off the proceeds of their knitting and weaving. And it was entirely due to the courage and persistence of such nuns (who, like Sister Theodoti, received no regular income from the Orthodox Church) that the establish-ment continued to exist even after its endowment had been sold

off in 1900. Theodoti Kolokotronis was herself the only survivor
from a dozen or so young women who took their vows some
time before the Second World War, their faded group photograph
pinned up, alongside other mementoes, in her day-room. She
lives in the building together with a close relative, Patir (Father)
Nektarios Papadakis, who serves as a priest in the nearby village
as well as in the monastery's own church. And now, I learned,
not only was she still in The Golden Stairway, but she was also
in better health, the crippling condition of her knees having been
alleviated by an operation carried out in Athens, with the result
that she could walk upright with much greater ease.

Thanking the carob-picking family for their kindness and their
excellent news, I moved on down the track, and fifteen or so
minutes later had the monastery itself in sight. Before walking
down to it, however, I decided to pause in a nearby kafeneion-
cum-bar. Still only about eleven-thirty in the morning, it seemed
a moment to draw breath, as well as to change my sweat-soaked
running vest before going in to see Theodoti. I drank a good deal
of lemonade, brought my journal up to date, and checked and
re-checked my sums.

The journey had taken me a fortnight – or just over thirteen and
a half days, to be precise, for the first and last of them each had
only a portion of the time available devoted to walking. As for the
distance covered, it was impossible to be accurate, given the frequent absence or errors of signposts, the inadequacies of the map,
and, above all, my frequent windings to and fro across the sides of
hills and mountains. The best figure I could come up with – and it
could have been out either way by as much as twenty miles, I think
– was just under 390 miles. So much had I added to the island's
directly measured length by my zig-zagging on a tactical level, so
to speak, but above all by the series of strategic swings, at right
angles to the east–west axis, that I had made in order to cross over
the mountain ranges that stood along the way.

I did not feel at all exhausted from all this, and apart from
the burden of my blisters I had experienced no aches or pains
throughout the trip. (The heat had doubtless helped in this
respect, and I had taken care to apply a herbal balm each evening

to the main joints that were bearing the strain.) Indeed, had it not been for that matter of the blisters, and for the fact that my boots, too, had all but had enough, I would readily have accepted a challenge to walk back in the reverse direction – though I would have wanted to vary the route for interest's sake.

My carob-picking family had driven up meanwhile, and had joined a group of friends who were already seated at a table across the other side of the terrace. We waved, and I could see that they were telling the others what I had been up to. One of the latter, a strong-faced woman in her forties, called across to me: 'Is it true that you have walked across all of Crete?' I said it was. Unhurriedly, and without another word, she pushed back her chair, got up, walked over to me, and shook me firmly by the hand. I recalled the old man on the mule outside Ayios Stephanos who had done the same thing all those miles before, and once again I was moved.

It was time I went down to see Theodoti. I waved goodbye to the family, slung my rucksack over one shoulder only (the abandon of it!), and descended the track to where it ended in a courtyard and parking area close beneath the monastery walls. There was a large, though ageing, Mercedes there, carefully positioned in the shade of the trees. Passing it, I climbed up the series of external stone stairs that took me to the main floor of the building, beside its church. The whiteness of the walls in the sunshine was almost too much for the eyes, and the sea below was its usual travel-poster blue. I turned sharp right as I emerged at the head of the stairway, came to the cool doorway of the day-room beyond, and there was Theodoti: more upright, indeed, than before, but otherwise seemingly unchanged: her dark brown eyes, framed by the black of her habit, glowing with vitality and intelligence; her voice, as she called out a welcome, rich with peace and certainty and the enjoyment of life.

Sipping a cold drink (there was raki to follow, of course), I explained the journey that I had just completed, where the bastouni came from, what I had been up to in the years since I had last visited the monastery, and so on. I broke off, though, when a man I did not know entered the room: a Frank like me, obviously, rather than a Greek, and of around my own age; a trifle stooped and dressed in clothes that looked to me, in my athletic semi-nakedness, to be far too hot for the climate, and that were certainly a trifle dishevelled. His face, however, reflected that of Theodoti in its manifestation of intelligence and good humour. He spoke to her in fluent, though accented, Greek, then switched effortlessly to English in order to introduce himself to me: Gotthold Müller; friend of Nektarios and Theodoti for twenty-five years; a frequent visitor to Crete, and Professor of Theology (what else could he have been? I observed, with such a Christian name) at the University of Würzburg.

Belatedly, I understood why the newcomer's questions to Theodoti had concerned the lay-out of a room. For my fellow professor had driven from Germany (the Mercedes in the courtyard was his), and was now staying on the northern shore of Crete between the monastery and Hania, in order to carry on with a series of repairs and improvements that he had been undertaking as a means of making the living-quarters of our mutual and esteemed friend less spartan, especially for those winter months when a bitter cold descends upon this remote and exposed extremity of the island. So there were doors to be fitted with draught-excluders, new shelving to be put up in order to save needless journeys into a freezing courtyard, and eventually – on a later visit – an electric heater to be installed in order to mitigate the severities of a bathroom clad only in chilled stone. Perhaps if I could wait for an hour or two, the Professor suggested, while he completed his tasks for the day, he would gladly give me a lift up to the main north-coast road about twenty-five miles away, where I could catch a bus to Hania and so begin my journey back to the East.

I would do more than that, I replied. I would join him in his labours. And so it was that the two of us set to work on the floor above the day-room, where the living-quarters of the monastery's inhabitants are sited. (The tools, screws, brackets, lengths of timber and so on that we needed were already there, having been brought from Germany in the boot of the Mercedes.) We must have looked an incongruous duo in our contrasting outfits, mine involving much bare brown leg and a stout, if weary, pair of walking boots; his more suitable for pottering around in at home, in the cooler north. It also occurred to me, as we sawed and hammered, that we were in one sense probably the most highly qualified pair of jobbing labourers in the Eastern Mediterranean at that moment, a thought that afforded us some amusement.

I will not pretend that the practical side of things proved to be entirely plain sailing. Gotthold's method of preparing a length of wood so that it could be added on to the bottom of a particularly ill-fitting door was to squint at the gap to be filled, squint in turn at the piece of timber in his hand, and then saw. If it then transpired that he had taken off too little, he would cut again along a new line; if he had taken off too much, then the piece of wood was replaced by another. Confidence he clearly possessed in abundance, but mine began to wilt a trifle. Moreover, I could not help noticing that he could never readily lay his hands on the particular tools or screws that he wanted, and that even while I sought to bring some vestiges of order to the pile of variegated ironware that lay on the stone flagging between us, it took only a couple of new operations on Gotthold's part to reduce matters to something close to chaos once more.

Eventually, I felt obliged to remonstrate. Would not a little measuring be in order, I suggested. I was far from being one of the number-crunching breed of social scientists myself, but if this was how theologians reached their conclusions – on matters, after all, of no little moment for the human species – were they not leaving an unnecessary degree of latitude for error? And again, how could we possibly see to it that the new European community of states and peoples functioned smoothly if those involved did not at least to some reassuring extent adhere to those patterns of behaviour that others had long come to expect of them? How could we forge ahead, challenging the Americans and defying the Japanese, if he, a German, insisted on operating with all the slapdash amateurism that could confidently be associated with the British, thus obliging me, in my turn, to play the methodical Teuton?

And so on. We had great fun imagining how various branches of academe other than our own might approach the tasks in question, as well as exchanging book titles like a pair of small boys sharing train numbers. And while shelves of a kind were being put up above Theodoti's bed and – eventually – that howling gap beneath her bathroom door was filled in, we were discovering that our political views, if not our respective approaches to carpentry, were very similar. Thus we laughed and grimaced over that need to live through the exercise of power which appeared to motivate a Kohl, and grew angry together over the obscenities of Thatcherism. We knew, I think, that we were embarking upon a valued friendship – on my part, with someone whose sensitivity and concern for others were striking. My views and feelings regarding the history of the German occupation of Crete remained unchanged, of course. But they did not differ at all from Gotthold's own, as he made clear. And as for the more diffuse, anti-German reflex that had begun to hover around my responses to the brutalised villages as I passed through them – a reflex, as I have suggested, that may also have owed something to my own childhood memories, and that was even beginning to override my subsequent and happy experiences with young German students – that now received its salutary antidote.[1]

Eventually, we decided that we could sustain our high level of craftmanship no longer that day, gathered up our tools, and descended the stairs to where a delighted Theodoti had prepared for us a simple but excellent cold meal. And now we were four,

---

[1] Perhaps there is a pale analogy here – the circumstances in the other case were entirely different, of course – with that remarkable episode related by Eric Newby in chapter eleven of his *Love and War in the Apennines* (London, 1971 and 1983). Sheltering with Italian peasants while on the run from the remorseless Germans and their local fascist allies in 1943, Newby, who had fallen asleep on a mountain-side at the time, was stumbled upon by an armed German officer. Recognising Newby for the escaped prisoner-of-war that he was, the German, in fluent English, engaged him in thoughtful conversation, advised him how best to avoid recapture, fiercely repudiated the policies and deeds of the Third Reich, and then continued his hunt for specimens of the local butterflies. In civilian life, Uberleutnant Frick was a professor at the University of Göttingen.

because Patir Nektarios came in to join us from his work in the fields, pulling on his somewhat soiled priest's robe over his trousers, vest, and sandals. His twinkling eyes, anarchic grey beard, and vast enjoyment of the jug of local wine that he and I shared between us (Gotthold had soon to drive) added a Chaucerian flavour to the occasion. There was much laughter around the table, Theodoti's being by far the most infectious. The spirit of all that is best in Crete lies here, too, I thought: not only in the proud shepherds of Zoniana, with their dancing and shooting; not only in a Kostas Manousakis, dispensing hospitality to a stranger on the mountainside above Kastamonitsa; not only in a Yannis Dafermos, puckishly shaping the verses that would take wing from his lira; but here, also, in this resolute, gentle, and infinitely compassionate woman.[1]

It was time to go, however, if I was to have any chance of catching my succession of buses back through Hania, Iraklion, and Ayios Nikolaos. We made plans for Gotthold and myself to meet up at the monastery the following year, there to resume our contribution to the art of home-improvement. We called back and forth to each other – Theodoti and Patir Nektarios looking down from a parapet above, Gotthold and I pausing in our descent to the courtyard and the Mercedes. 'Good journey!' 'Till next year!' 'Many thanks again!'

The two of us stowed away the tools and their accompanying odds and ends in the boot of the car. I got into the front, undid the laces of my boots, checked an impulse to think about the route ahead, and leaned back against the soft, worn leather of the seat. The rocks and heat of the mountain slopes began to seem far away. Then Gotthold drove us off, past the few, simple houses, up the long, stony track, and away for the time being.

---

[1] During the following summer I stayed overnight at the monastery – though, alas, Gotthold was prevented by ill-health from attending the reunion. On this occasion I sat in on the evening service that Father Nektarios, assisted by Sister Theodoti, conducted in the church. There were three of us in the congregation: the old man and old woman who helped out around the monastery, and myself. By the time the lengthy service was drawing to a close it had grown dark outside, and the candles within cast the softest of shadows. Then the five of us sat down to supper together. My agnosticism remained intact, but I had found it an affecting occasion which helped place and keep problems in their proper perspective.

Bibliographical note

There are guide-books aplenty on Crete. But anyone wishing to begin a serious study of the island's distant past should still consult, despite subsequent findings, J. D. S. Pendlebury, *The Archaeology of Crete: An Introduction* (London, 1939/1967), which is also indispensable for its 'feel' for the actual countryside of Crete, which Pendlebury endlessly traversed. For a commentary on Pendlebury himself, and on the archaeological community that surrounded Sir Arthur Evans and his work at Knossos, Dilys Powell's *The Villa Ariadne* (Athens, 1982) is excellent, and provides as well insights into rural, pre-tourist Cretan society. On Minoan and Dorian Crete there are three helpful volumes by R. F. Willetts: *Ancient Crete: A Social History* (London, 1965); *Everyday Life in Ancient Crete* (London, 1969); *The Civilization of Ancient Crete* (London, 1977). A work of great erudition that is also informed by a love of the island and its people is P. Faure's *La Vie Quotidienne En Crète Au Temps De Minos* (Paris, 1973).

The most up-to-date and detailed guide to the archaeological and historical sites of Crete is Stergios Spanakis' Η ΚΡΗΤΗ: ΤΟΥΡΙΣΤΙΚΟΣ ΙΣΤΟΡΙΚΟΣ ΑΡΧΑΙΟΛΟΓΙΚΟΣ: ΟΔΗΓΟΣ (Iraklion, n.d.), which is in two volumes, only the first of which, on the eastern half of the island, has been translated into English as *Crete: A Guide to Travel, History, and Archaeology* (Iraklion, n.d.).

A personal, essay-like survey of Cretan history and society is provided in M. L. Smith's *The Great Island: A Study of Crete* (London, 1965). And a detailed, anthropological study of life in a single mountain village, to which I have referred extensively in connection with Zoniana, is M. Herzfeld's *The Poetics of Manhood: Contest and Identity in a Cretan Mountain Village* (Princeton, NJ, 1985).

I have also drawn on studies about, or the original works of, various English-speaking visitors to Crete down the centuries. My debt in this regard concerning the pre-nineteenth century travellers is to an article by P. Warren, '16th, 17th and 18th Century British Travellers in Crete' in *Κρητικα Χρονικα*, 1972, pp. 65–92. Thereafter I have drawn extensively on R. Pashley, *Travels in Crete* (2 vols, London, 1837); R. Fowler (ed.), *Edward Lear: The Cretan Journal* (Athens, 1985); T. A. B. Spratt, *Travels and Researches in Crete* (2 vols, London, 1865), and the first-hand account by the US Consul, W. J. Stillman, *The Cretan Insurrection of 1866–7–8* (New York, 1874).

Concerning the history of the island during the Second World War, the numerous previous studies of the fighting in 1941 have recently been superseded by A. Beevor's *Crete: The Battle and the Resistance* (London, 1991). From the Cretans' own point of view, George Psychoundakis' *The Cretan Runner* (trans. Patrick Leigh Fermor, London, 1955/1978) is stirring and indispensable. On the British side, the memoirs of participants in the island's resistance include A. M. Rendel, *Appointment in Crete: The Story of a British Agent* (London, 1953); while on a single and celebrated episode there is W. S. Moss, *Ill Met By Moonlight: The Abduction of General Kreipe* (Athens, 1958). The remarkable agent Xan Fielding wrote a valuable account of his return to the area of the White Mountains in 1952 in *The Stronghold: An Account of the Four Seasons in Crete* (London, 1953), while on the life and death of the New Zealander, Dudley Perkins, there is M. Elliott, *Vasili, the Lion of Crete* (Auckland, 1987). Regarding the travails and attractions of post-war Greece as a whole, I have made reference to K. Andrews, *The Flight of Ikaros: Travels in Greece During the Civil War* (London, 1984).

I am told by Gotthold Müller that a superb study of Cretan society, by a Cretan, is Vassilios Vuidaskis' *Tradition und sozialer Wandel auf der Insel Kreta* (Meisenheim, 1982).

And I obtained too late to make use of in the present book the fascinating series of essays edited by David Holton, *Literature and Society in Renaissance Crete* (Cambridge, 1991).

Index

Index